L.L. BEAN

OUTDOOR

KNOTS

HANDBOOK

Written and illustrated by Peter Owen
Designed and produced by HB Design

Printed in Canada

10 9 8 7 6 5 4 3 2 1

Library of Congress Cataloging-in-Publication Data

Owen, Peter, 1950–
      L.L. Bean outdoor knots handbook / Peter Owen.
            p. cm.
      Includes index.
      ISBN 1-55821-871-8 (pb)
      1. Knots and splices. I. Title
      VM533.094323 1999
      623.88'82—dc21   99-23385
                                                                    CIP

L.L. BEAN
OUTDOOR
KNOTS
HANDBOOK

PETER OWEN

The Lyons Press

CONTENTS

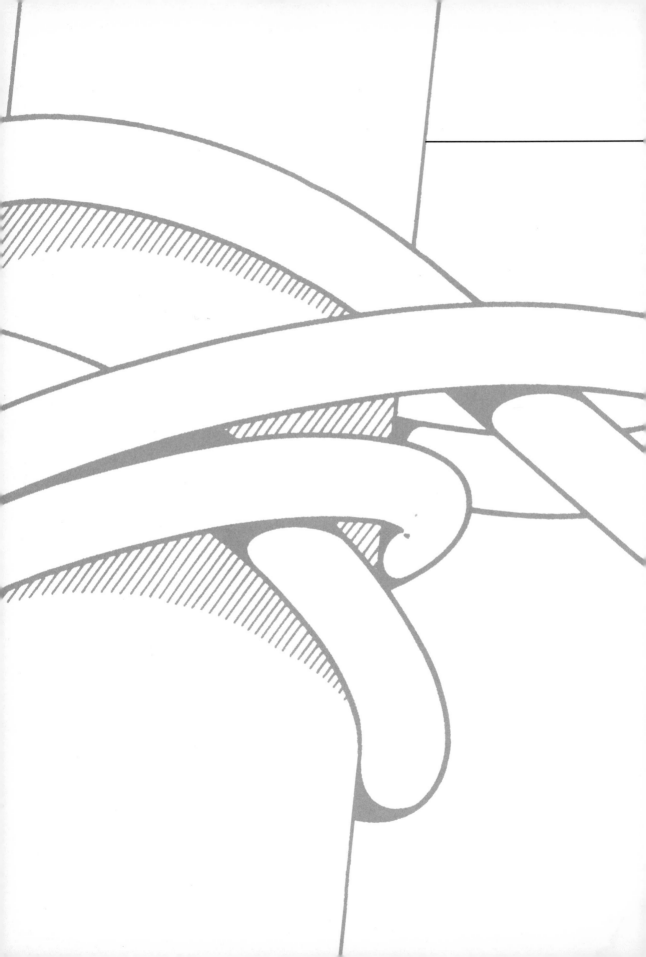

INTRODUCTION

INTRODUCTION

A knot is a connection in a line, cord, or piece of rope. It can be in the line itself or between two lines; it can serve to attach something to a line or even a purely decorative purpose. Learning how to form a knot properly and knowing which knot to use for a given purpose is essential to the safety and enjoyment of many outdoor pursuits—and could mean the difference between life and death.

The term *outdoor pursuits* encompasses a huge range of activities, many of which have seen some revolutionary changes in recent years, especially in the area of equipment. But the one component that has changed very little over time and is still totally necessary for almost all forms of outdoor pursuits is the knot. Natural fiber ropes and lines have been almost totally replaced by artificial fiber ropes and lines, but natural fiber ropes are still favored by some people and have distinct advantages, especially when it comes to decorative knotting.

The **L.L. Bean Outdoor Knots Handbook** gives you the opportunity, through clear instructions and easy-to-follow, step-by-step illustrations, to master 90 classic outdoor knots, including specialist knots for sailing, boating, climbing, caving, and fishing. The knots, meticulously explained and described, are divided into

INTRODUCTION

several distinct groups, each of which is used for different purposes. Within each group there are many variations, but it is not necessary to know every one; four or five should be sufficient. The most important thing is selecting the right knot for the job.

Finally, remember that mastering anything takes practice, and tying knots is no exception. The only way to learn how to tie a specific knot is in a relaxed atmosphere, not halfway up a mountain or out at sea in a storm. Practice knots over and over until the movements become automatic. Your own life, or the lives of others, may depend on it, so you must have the skill and confidence to be able to tie the knots you need correctly and without hesitation or doubt — no matter what the situation or how difficult the conditions.

Figure-eight loop (page 50)

ROPE
MANUFACTURE

Rope is manufactured in either natural or artificial fibers that can be twisted or braided, and is available in a wide variety of sizes. Rope size can be measured by circumference or diameter, and may be designated by a term such as *twine* (a thin line for various uses).

Traditionally, rope was made by twisting fibers of natural materials together. The most commonly used materials were manila, sisal, coir, hemp, flax, and cotton. The fibers were twisted first into yarn, then into strands, and finally into rope, in a process called laying up. Examine a piece of ordinary three-strand rope and you will notice that the strands go up and to the right, like a corkscrew. It has been "laid" right-handed. When the rope was made the fibers were twisted together to form right-hand yarn, the yarn was then twisted in the opposite direction to form left-hand strands, and these were twisted to form right-laid rope. If you uncoil one strand you can clearly see it is laid up left-handed, or twisted the opposite way to the whole rope. This is a vital principle of traditional rope making. Even with one strand removed, the other two strands cling together, leaving a groove where the missing strand should be. It is the alternate twisting that creates the tension that holds the rope together and gives it strength.

NATURAL FIBER
ROPE

For thousands of years, until shortages during World War II led to the development of man-made fibers, rope was made from natural materials—cotton and flax for manageability, coir and sisal for cheapness, manila and hemp for strength.

Natural fiber rope is normally three-strand and right-laid. Four-strand, left-laid rope is much rarer and 10 percent weaker—adding further strands does not increase strength. Cable-laid line (a nine-strand cable laid up left-handed from three-strand ropes) is 40 percent weaker than hawser-laid (three-strand) rope of the same diameter.

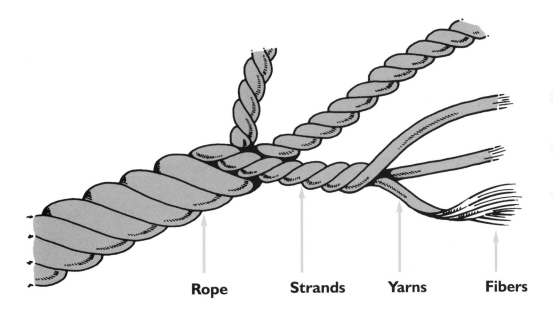

Rope   **Strands**   **Yarns**   **Fibers**

Three-strand natural fiber rope

NATURAL FIBER
ROPE

Natural fibers are only as long as the plant from which they were derived allows; the ends of these individual fibers (known as staples) are what give natural rope its hairy, rough appearance. This gives them better traction and resistance than smooth man-made fibers. However, natural fibers have many disadvantages. They lack elasticity; they swell and become heavy when wet, making knots difficult to untie. They attract mildew and will rot if not stored properly, and they can be weakened and made brittle by strong sunlight, chemicals, and salt.

Nowadays natural fiber rope is used less often for outdoor pursuits, but for decorative purposes many still prefer vegetable fibers for their traditional appearance and the beauty of their natural colors and textures.

ARTIFICIAL FIBER ROPE

Artificial or synthetic materials have almost completely replaced natural fibers in the manufacture of rope. Man-made filaments can be spun to run the whole length of a line, do not vary in thickness, and do not have to be twisted together to make them cohere. This gives them superior strength.

Nylon, first produced in 1938 for domestic use, was the first man-made material to be used in this way. Since then a range of artificial ropes has been developed to meet different needs, but they all share certain characteristics. Size for size they are lighter, stronger, and cheaper than their natural counterparts. They do not rot or mildew and are not affected by salt water. They are resistant to sunlight, chemicals, oil, gasoline, and most common solvents. They absorb less water than natural fiber ropes, and so their wet breaking strain remains constant. They can also be made in a range of colors.

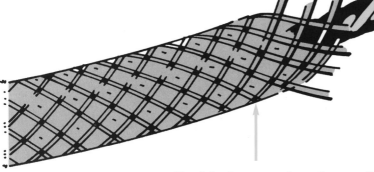

Braided outer sheath   **Inner core**

Braided artificial fiber rope

ARTIFICIAL FIBER
ROPE

Color-coded ropes make for instant recognition of lines of different functions. In addition, artificial ropes have high tensile strength, are capable of absorbing shocks, and have excellent load-bearing qualities.

Nylon (polyamide) fibers make ropes that are both strong and elastic, giving them outstanding capacity for absorbing shock loads. They are good for towing and, because they do not rot or float, are particularly useful in sailing. One big advantage that climbers and sailors have found with this type of rope is that it is far more comfortable to hold and use than natural fiber rope.

Polyester (Dacron) ropes are nearly as strong as nylon and stretch very little. They do not float and are highly resistant to wear and weathering, so they are widely used in sailing and boating. Polyester is also used in small sizes for twine.

Polypropylene (polyethylene) is not as strong as nylon or polyester but it does make a good, inexpensive, all-purpose rope. Its one main advantage is that it is the only fiber that floats, thus making it particularly suitable for water-ski tow ropes and rescue lines. Floating does mean, however, that it may be caught in or cut by a propeller.

Artificial ropes are constantly being developed and improved. It is always worth checking with your local chandler or specialist rope supplier about any new products coming onto the market for outdoor pursuits.

Artificial fiber ropes do have some disadvantages, the main one being that they melt when heated. Even the friction generated when one rope rubs against another may be enough to cause damage, so it is vital to check your ropes regularly. Use plastic tubing to protect sections of artificial rope that you know will be subject to friction. It is also possible for heat friction to fuse knotted rope together so that it is impossible to untie the knot. Another disadvantage is that artificial ropes made of continuous filaments are so smooth that knots slip and come undone. You may need to secure knots with additional knots or seizings.

Artificial rope can be laid up or twisted like natural fiber rope, or it can be formed into braided rope with an outer sheath of 16 or more strands surrounding a central core that is either braided and hollow or made up of solid parallel, or slightly twisted, filaments. Braided rope is softer, more flexible, and quite a lot stronger.

Laid-up rope, made of thick multifilaments tightly twisted together, may be very resistant to wear — but it can also be difficult to tie, and knots may not hold well. Do not buy a rope that is too stiff. Similarly, be wary of twisted rope that is very soft.

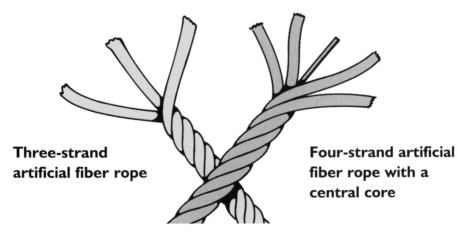

Three-strand artificial fiber rope

Four-strand artificial fiber rope with a central core

Twisted artificial fiber rope

LOOKING AFTER
ROPE

Rope is sturdy material, but it is expensive, so it's worth looking after properly. Caring for rope will help maintain its strength and prolong its life. Avoid dragging it over rough, sharp edges, or dirty, gritty surfaces where particles could get into the rope and damage it. Do not walk on rope or force it into harsh kinks. Inspect it regularly and wash off dirt, grit, and oil. Coil rope carefully and always make sure it is dry before coiling, even if it is artificial fiber rope. If it has been in salt water, rinse thoroughly to remove all salt deposits.
Wash all ropes in a mild detergent, removing oil or tar stains with gasoline or trichloroethylene.

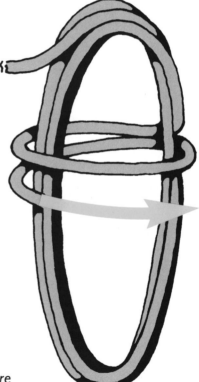

Coiling a rope will ensure that it will be immediately to hand and untangled when required.

LOOKING AFTER
ROPE

If you repeatedly tie knots in one section of rope, that section will weaken. The tighter the nip or the sharper the curve, the greater the chances that the rope will break; if it does, it will part immediately outside the knot.

Finally, never use two ropes of different materials together, because only the more rigid of the two will work under strain.

SELECTING
KNOTS

The main factor to consider when selecting one knot above another is the relative strengths of the knots. This is particularly important for mountaineers and climbers, but knot strength is also something sailors need to take into consideration. Other factors influencing choice will be the speed and ease with which a knot can be tied, the size of the finished knot, and its reliability.

Climbers' knots tend to be bulky, with several wrapping turns to absorb the strain and prevent the rope from being weakened unnecessarily. It is very important for climbers to check their knots regularly, especially if the rope they are using is at all stiff. Stiff rope is more difficult to tie than very flexible line, and the knots in it may be less secure.

Figure-eight bend (page 79)

Anglers' knots are similar to those used by climbers, but much smaller and generally tied in thin monofilament line. They also need strength and reliability of wrapping turns if they are to secure their catch and not lose valuable tackle.

Being able to untie a knot is as important as knowing how to tie it. Usually you should untie knots after you have used them.

SELECTING KNOTS

This is made easier if you have chosen a suitable knot in the first place and tied it correctly. If you want to be able to untie a knot quickly, introduce a draw-loop. The knot will be no less strong and secure, but it can be undone with a single tug. Knots like the clove hitch are efficient and reliable but disappear as soon as they are slipped off their foundation.

As you select the knot for your job, remember that knots perform differently under different sorts of strain. Some knots remain very strong while subjected to steady loading but will slip and even fall apart if submitted to intermittent jerking. These knots, although strong, are insecure and should not be used in situations where they might come under sudden violent stress.

Finally, you should remember that knots reduce the breaking strain of any line, whatever the material, by 5 to 20 percent. Knots slip just before they break, but if a knot is correctly tied and drawn as tight as possible, it will withstand a much greater strain before it begins to slip.

Spade-end knot (page 134)

HOW TO
USE THIS BOOK

The diagrams accompanying the descriptions of the knots are intended to be self-explanatory. Written instructions and special tying techniques and methods will accompany the more complex knots. There are arrows to show the directions in which you should push or pull the working ends of the rope or line. The dotted lines indicate intermediate positions of the rope. In many of the illustrations lines are shown faded out or cut short for clarity. When tying the knot you should always have a working end sufficient to complete it. The amount of working end required can often be calculated by looking at the illustration of the finished knot. Always follow the order shown of going over or under a length of line; reversing or changing this order could result in a completely different knot, which might well be unstable and unsafe.

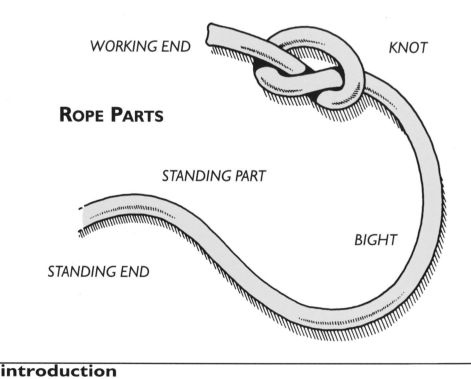

WORKING END KNOT

ROPE PARTS

STANDING PART

BIGHT

STANDING END

KNOT USAGE SYMBOLS

The symbols above the knots show the activities for which they are best or most commonly used.

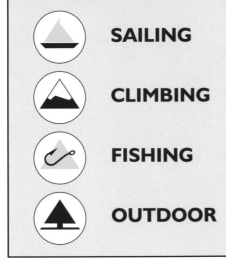

SAILING

CLIMBING

FISHING

OUTDOOR

WARNING

Friction-generated heat may cause artificial fiber rope to weaken and break without warning (see pages 14 and 15). Extreme caution should be exercised, especially by rock climbers, mountaineers, and cavers, when using artificial fiber rope in situations that may cause friction damage. The result could be fatal.

ROPE
ENDS

A slowly unraveling rope with frayed ends is annoying, wasteful, and in some cases dangerous. But a rope with correctly sealed ends is safe, neat, and makes knots significantly easier to tie.

Artificial fiber ropes are now widely used in sailing and have many advantages, one of them being that the rope ends can be quickly and efficiently heat-sealed to prevent them from fraying. But natural fiber ropes are still used, and if left unseized, the ends will fray. A secure and easy way to prevent this is by whipping the ends. Use vegetable fiber twine or waxed polyester twine, and always bind against the lay.

COMMON
WHIPPING

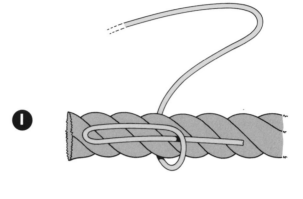

This easily tied and practical whipping is, as its name suggests, one of the most widely used forms of whipping.

But it should be remembered that if the rope end frequently becomes wet, most whipping twines will swell and stretch. This can lead to the whipping loosening and slipping off. For rope ends that are subject to becoming wet, this should be seen as only a temporary whipping.

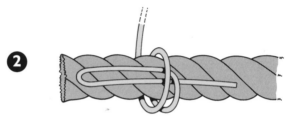

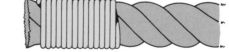

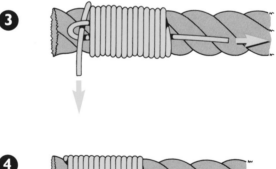

Trim the loose ends of the whipping twine and make neat the rope strand ends. With artificial ropes, the strand ends can be heat-sealed.

1

To ensure that the knotted end of the twine is held securely, push the needle through the center of a strand.

This durable and reliable whipping is especially suited to twisted natural fiber rope, but can also be tied on braided or artificial fiber ropes.

2

Make the required number of turns toward the rope end and then push the needle behind one of the rope strands.

It will stand up well to friction, so it can be employed for heavy usage. You will need a needle with an eye big enough to take whipping twine. Special sail maker's needles are available for this purpose.

3

Follow the gap between the strands down to the lower end of the whipping. Insert the needle so that it exits from the next gap and follow back to the top of the whipping. Continue to create this diagonal line running down each gap.

4

To finish, pull the twine under the whipping and trim the loose ends. If the rope is braided rather than twisted, the diagonal lines can still be added.

SNAKED
WHIPPING

This decorative and highly effective whipping is suited to large-diameter ropes; it can prove difficult to tie on thinner ropes.

It is important with all whipping, and especially snaked whipping, to make sure that each turn is pulled as tight as possible. Also, to make the snaking less likely to slip, as you pass the needle under the whipping, pick up a few fibers of the rope itself. The decorative appearance of this whipping makes it ideal for ropes that are left out on show or on board.

❶

Start in the same way as for palm & needle whipping (see page 25). To ensure that the knotted end of the twine is held securely, push the needle through the center of a strand.

❷

Make the required number of turns away from the rope end and then push the needle through the rope, keeping the turns tight.

❸

Create the snaked pattern using the two end strands of the whipping to secure the diagonal crosses.

❹

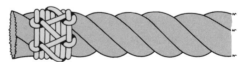

To finish, knot the twine with two half hitches, push the hitches under the whipping, and trim the loose ends.

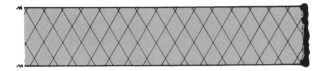

Heat-sealed synthetic rope

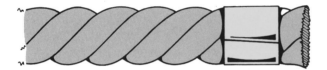

Rope sealed with adhesive or electrical tape

Rope sealed with a stopper knot

Apart from whipping the ends of rope, there are three other options to consider to seal ends.

All synthetic rope ends can be sealed using heat. When you buy synthetic rope from chandlers, they will cut it to the required length using an electrically heated knife, which gives a neat, sharp edge. When you cut synthetic rope yourself, use a sharp knife and then melt the end with a cigarette lighter or on an electric burner.

A quick and efficient method of creating a temporary seal is to use ordinary adhesive or electrical tape. And finally, on small stuff (any rope whose circumference is less than 1 inch), a simple stopper knot will provide an effective seal.

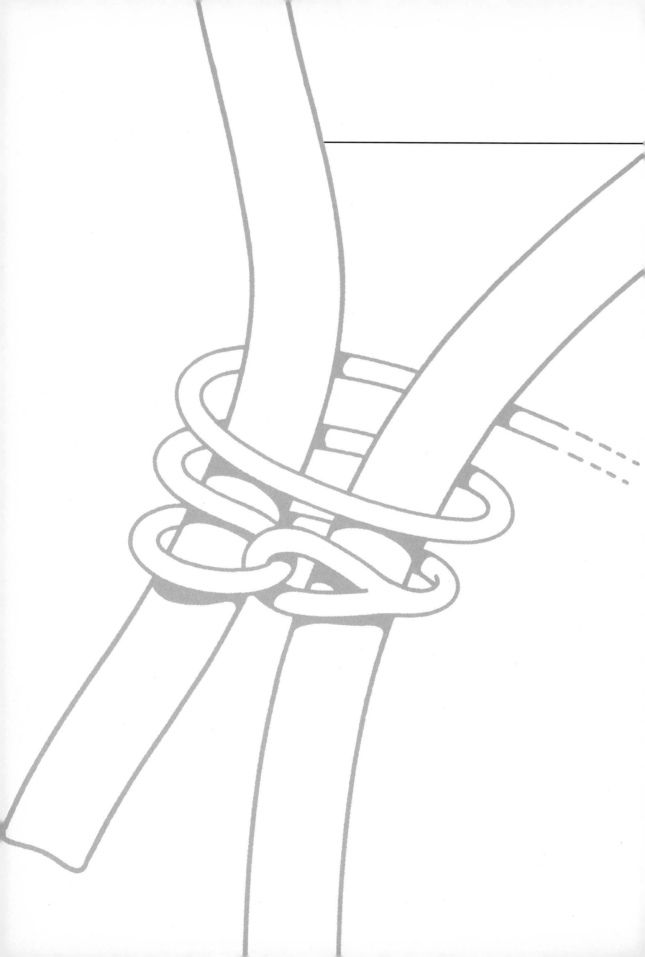

SEIZINGS

A seizing is used to bind two ropes together. The same thickness and type of twine or small stuff used for whipping is generally applicable for seizing.

Seizing can be used to bind two separate parts of rope together, but it is most widely used to bind the same piece of rope together to form an eye.

This simple form of seizing is good for light loads and to temporarily bind two pieces of rope together.

For this type of seizing, use twine or thin line that has been prepared with a small eye at one end.

Prepare the seizing twine by forming a small eye in one end. This is done by opening up the strands and tucking the twine end through a couple of times.

1

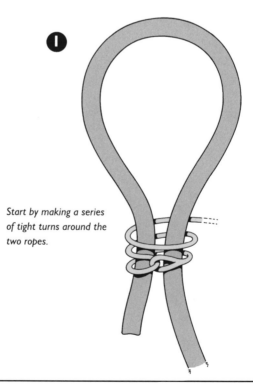

Start by making a series of tight turns around the two ropes.

2

When sufficient turns have been
made, thread the twine down
between the two ropes and make
a series of turns around the
seizing at a 90-degree angle to
the original turns.

3

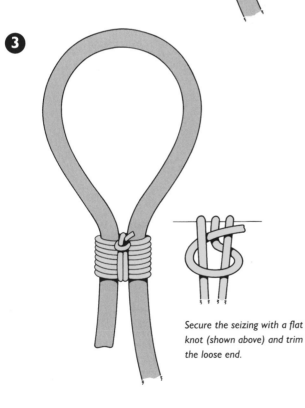

Secure the seizing with a flat
knot (shown above) and trim
the loose end.

This method of seizing creates a strong grip on the rope, making it suitable for heavy loads.

It is particularly useful for making eyes in the end of ropes. I recommend that you use a sail maker's needle to thread the twine through the rope.

1

Knot the end of the twine and thread it through one of the ropes. Take the twine up to the point that the seizing will finish and insert the needle back through the first rope, across, and out of the second rope.

2

Return to the starting point and insert the needle through the second rope. Pull the twine tight, continue, and finish in exactly the same way as for flat seizing (see page 30).

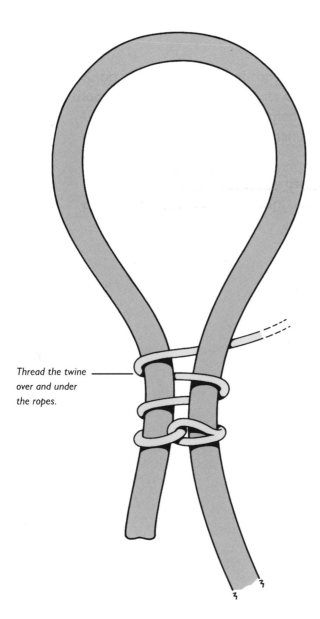

Thread the twine over and under the ropes.

This form of seizing should be used if the seized rope parts will be subject to excessive, uneven, or sideways loading.

Instead of making complete turns, thread the twine over and under the ropes. This will substantially strengthen the seizing. Racking can be applied to flat seizing (see page 30) and palm & needle seizing (see opposite).

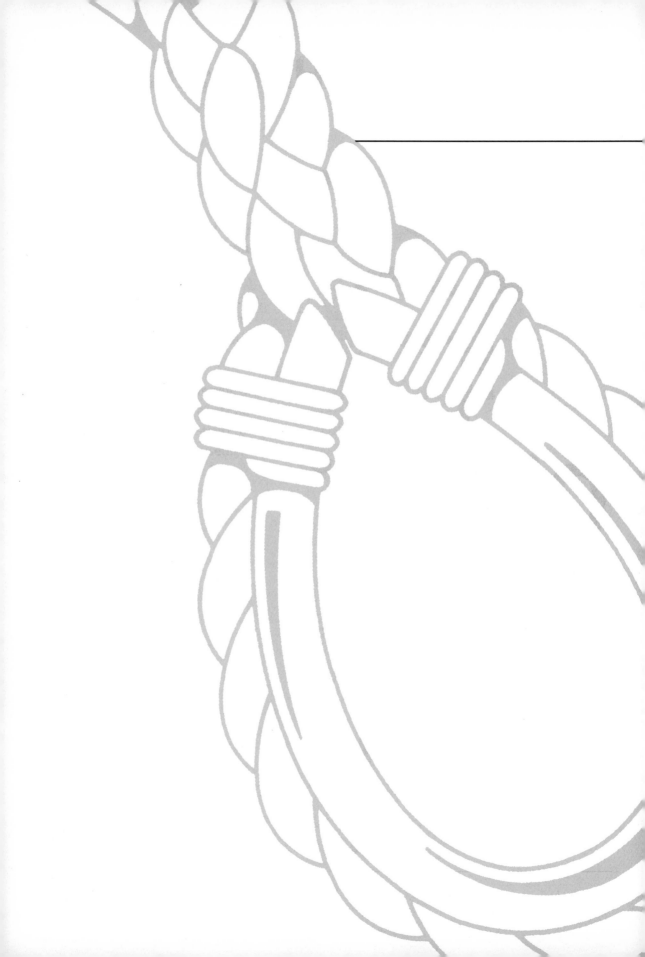

SPLICINGS

Splicing is a method of joining rope to itself or to another rope by interweaving the separate strands. It is a very reliable method and one that every sailor should know.

If you encounter difficulty in separating rope strands, use a fid. Most ropework, and especially splicing, benefits from being worked into shape; this can be done by rolling it underfoot or by using a wooden mallet or rubber-faced hammer. All the examples covered in this chapter are illustrated with the most commonly used three-strand rope.

This is one of the most widely used splices in the sailing world.

It is also known as Spanish whipping. It creates a decorative and practical end to a rope and, unlike whipping, it becomes firmer and stronger with time.

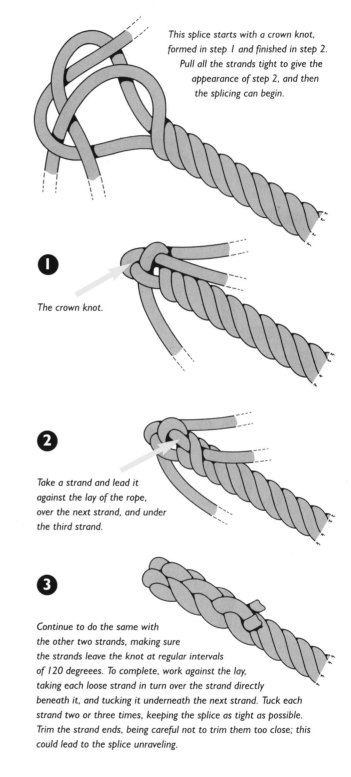

This splice starts with a crown knot, formed in step 1 and finished in step 2. Pull all the strands tight to give the appearance of step 2, and then the splicing can begin.

1

The crown knot.

2

Take a strand and lead it against the lay of the rope, over the next strand, and under the third strand.

3

Continue to do the same with the other two strands, making sure the strands leave the knot at regular intervals of 120 degreees. To complete, work against the lay, taking each loose strand in turn over the strand directly beneath it, and tucking it underneath the next strand. Tuck each strand two or three times, keeping the splice as tight as possible. Trim the strand ends, being careful not to trim them too close; this could lead to the splice unraveling.

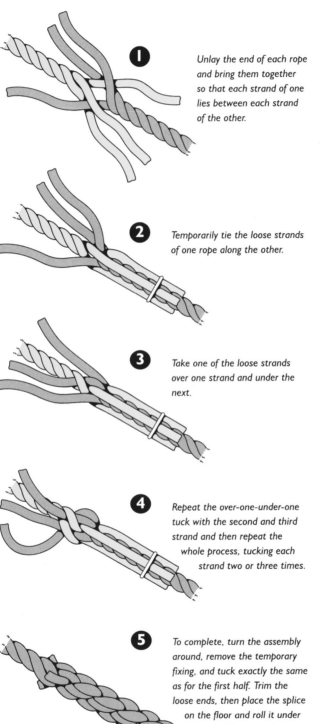

1 Unlay the end of each rope and bring them together so that each strand of one lies between each strand of the other.

2 Temporarily tie the loose strands of one rope along the other.

3 Take one of the loose strands over one strand and under the next.

4 Repeat the over-one-under-one tuck with the second and third strand and then repeat the whole process, tucking each strand two or three times.

5 To complete, turn the assembly around, remove the temporary fixing, and tuck exactly the same as for the first half. Trim the loose ends, then place the splice on the floor and roll it under your shoe to make it uniformly round.

This splice provides the ideal solution for permanently joining the ends of two ropes with little loss of strength.

It can also be successfully used to repair a break in a line.

This is one of the most important sailing knots and one that every sailor should learn.

You will always need eyes in the end of your ropes, and the eye splice is the most reliable way of achieving this.

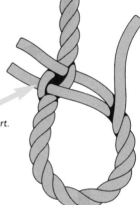

1 Unlay the end of the rope and form an eye. Tuck one of the loose strands under a strand in the standing part.

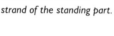

2 Thread the second strand under the next strand of the standing part.

3 Now turn the eye around and tuck the third strand under the only strand in the standing part that has not been used.

4 To complete, repeat the process, putting in two more tucks for each strand, making sure the splice is kept as tight as possible. Trim the loose ends and roll the splice between your hands to make it uniformly round.

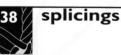

WITH THIMBLE

If subject to heavy use and chafing, an eye splice can be reinforced and strengthened with a thimble.

Thimbles are made from various metals or plastic and are available in a wide variety of sizes. The splice can be either tied around or stretched over a thimble.

Whipping that is kept well away from the working surface will secure a loose thimble.

Thimble

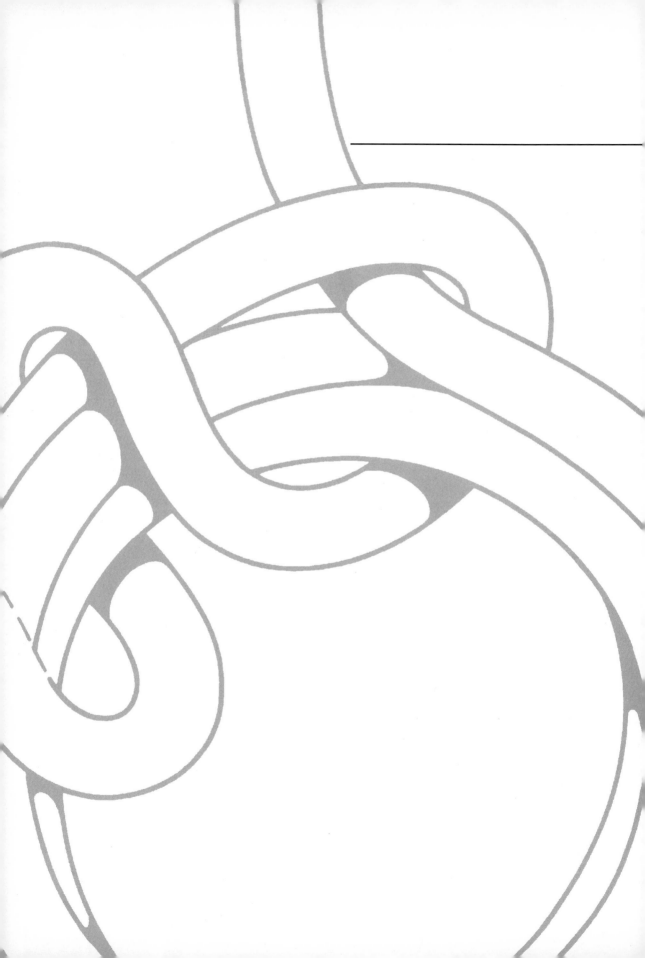

STOPPER
KNOTS

Stopper knots, as their name suggests, are used to prevent the ends of a rope or line from slipping through an eye, loop, or hole. They can be used to bind the end of a line so that it will not unravel, and can also be used decoratively. At sea they are used to weight lines as well as at the ends of running rigging.

The most important knot of this type is the overhand. This is the simplest, and perhaps the oldest, knot known to man and is used as a basis for countless others.

OVERHAND KNOT

Also known as the thumb knot, this knot forms the basis for many others.

It is used in its own right as a stopper knot, and is also tied at regular intervals along lines to make them easy to grip. If a line develops an unwanted overhand knot, undo it immediately, as this knot is very difficult to untie, especially when wet.

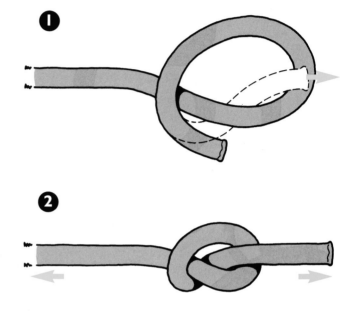

❶

❷

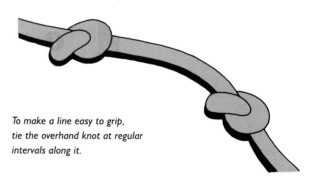

To make a line easy to grip, tie the overhand knot at regular intervals along it.

❶

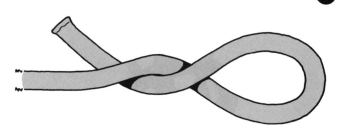

This knot's name comes from its characteristic shape. It is the most important stopper knot for sailors, used on running rigging. (It is also known as the Flemish knot or Savoy knot.)

The knot is made in the end of the line, with the upper loop around the standing part and the lower loop around the working end. When tying this knot you should leave a tail on the working end. This will enable you to grasp the knot should it become jammed.

❷

❸

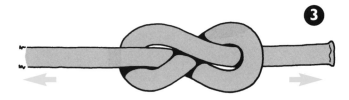

1

This knot is also known as the blood knot, and it earned that name because it was the knot used to weight the ends of the lashes in cat-o'-nine-tails, the whip used historically to flog soldiers, sailors, and criminals. Its main sailing uses are as a weighting or stopper knot made with small-diameter line.

When tying the knot, keep the loop open and slack as you make the turns and gently pull on both ends at the same time, twisting the two ends in opposite directions. Like many stopper knots, this knot is difficult to untie when the line is wet.

2

3

4

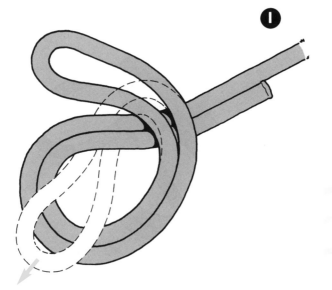

1

This knot is useful if a stopper with more bulk is required.

It is very difficult to untie, but it is the loop used instinctively by most people if they need to fasten a knot in the end of a piece of string and it does not have to be untied again.

2

 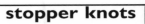

When a heavy line is thrown from boat to shore or to another vessel, a heaving line knot is used.

The heavy line is attached to a heaving line, a lighter line that is thrown across the gap first so the heavier line can be drawn behind it. The heaving line knot is tied in the end of this lighter line to give it weight and aid in throwing. Heaving lines are usually $1/2$ to $3/4$ inch in diameter and may be up to 80 feet long. They should float, be flexible, and be strong enough to bear a man's weight.

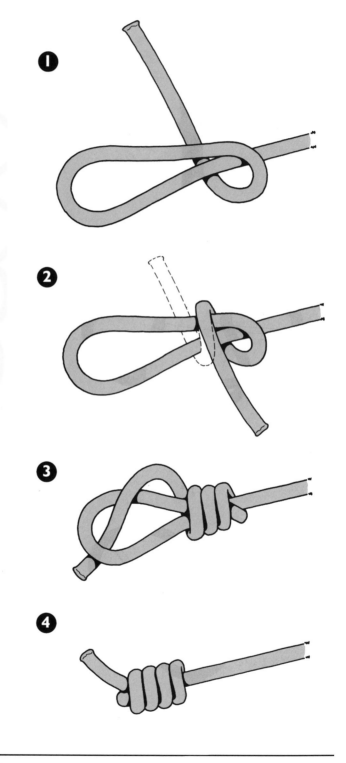

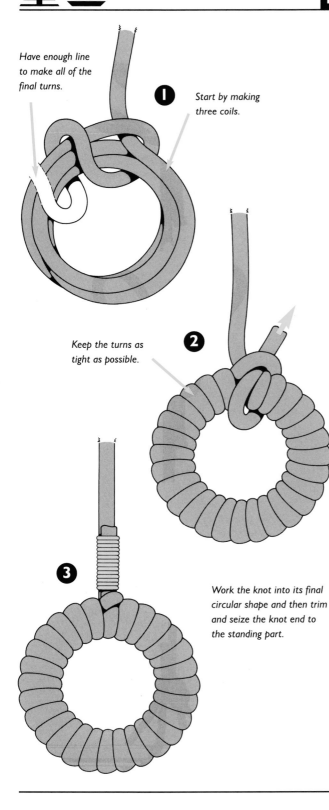

Have enough line to make all of the final turns.

1 *Start by making three coils.*

Keep the turns as tight as possible.

2

3

Work the knot into its final circular shape and then trim and seize the knot end to the standing part.

This decorative heaving line knot has the obvious advantages that other lines can be easily tied to it, and it can be hooked on or over objects.

The weight of this knot can be increased by wrapping a narrow strip of sheet lead around the original three coils before making the final turns. The doughnut also has a very useful secondary use: When it is tied in small material without the sheet lead, it can be used at the end of any cord that you need to pull.

LOOPS

Knots made in the end of rope by folding it back into an eye or loop and then knotting it to its own standing part are called loops. Unlike hitches, which are formed around an object and follow its shape, loops are made in the hand, generally to drop over an object.

Loops are the most commonly used group of sailing knots, and are particularly important to sailors.

FIGURE-EIGHT
LOOP

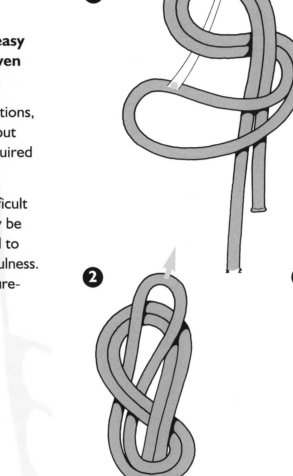

This knot is relatively easy to tie and stays tied, even when stiff rope is used.

It has many sailing applications, especially when a quick, but strong, eye or loop is required at the end of a rope.

Its disadvantages—it is difficult to adjust and cannot easily be untied after loading—tend to be outweighed by its usefulness. It is also known as the figure-eight on the bight.

①

This variation of the figure-eight loop is widely used in climbing for tying onto the rope and for anchoring nonclimbing members to a team.

A stopper knot should be added when you're using the threaded figure-eight loop to tie onto a line.

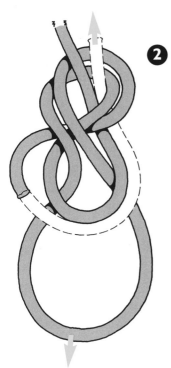

②

③

A stopper knot must be added when the threaded figure-eight loop is used to tie on a line.

loops **51**

PERFECTION
LOOP

The perfection loop is often used by fishermen and campers in a variety of ways, for hanging objects and securing lines to poles or pegs.

Also called the angler's loop, its advantages are that it is easy to tie, does not slide, and is very strong and stable. It is, however, rather bulky, which makes it more suited to tying in fishing line or fine synthetic line. The perfection loop is also difficult to untie and prone to jam, which makes it unsuitable for use at sea.

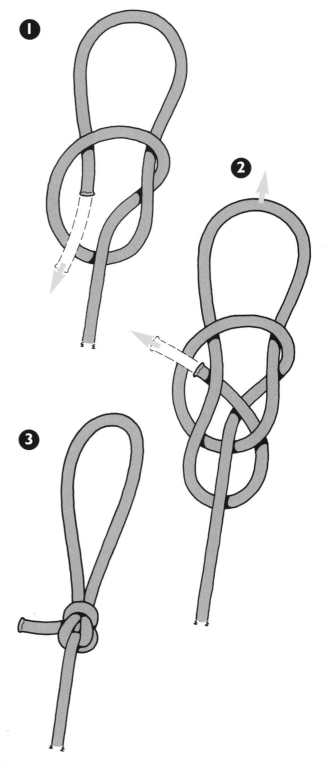

1

2

3

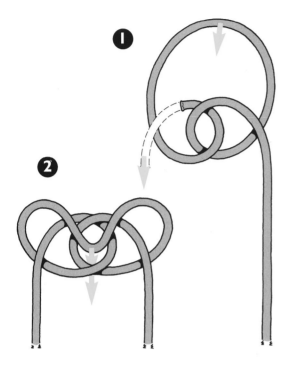

This knot is used by climbers and mountaineers. It fits around the chest and, because it is symmetrical, holds equally well whichever end is held.

It can be tied quickly, unties easily, and does not slip; the loop does not shrink when the knot is tightened. Its major disadvantage is that it is difficult to tie; the increased use of the Italian hitch (see page 97) has meant that the alpine butterfly knot has lost some of its popularity.

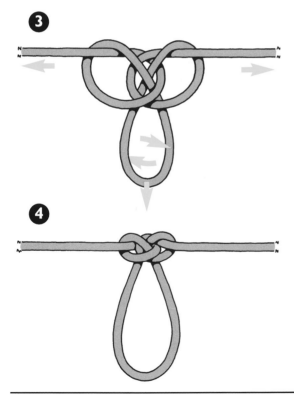

The bowline is one of the best-known and most widely used knots and is particularly important to sailors.

It is tied to form a fixed loop at the end of a line or to attach a rope to an object. It has many sailing applications, including use on running rigging and for hoisting, joining, and salvage work.

The bowline is simple to tie, strong, and stable. Its main advantages are that it does not slip or come loose, even in polypropylene ropes that allow other knots to slip. It is also quick and easy to untie, even when the line is under tension, by pushing forward the bight that encircles the standing part of the line.

For extra security, finish the bowline off with a stopper knot or an extra half hitch.

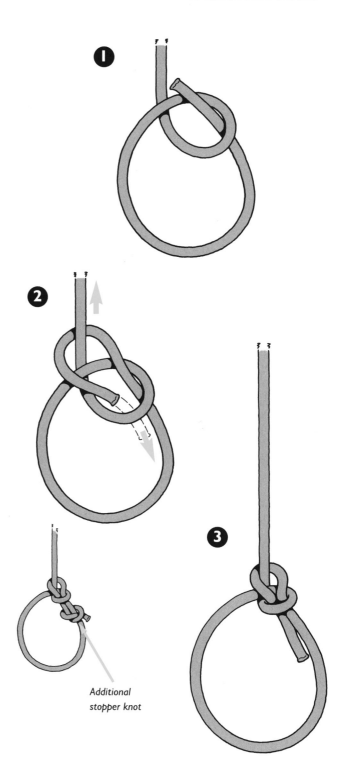

Additional stopper knot

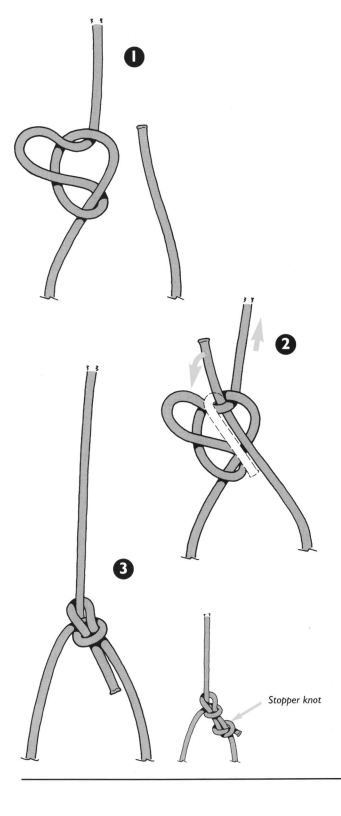

A climber's bowline is also known as a bulin knot. It is used as a safety measure during ascents, when it is clipped into a carabiner.

Climbers also tie this knot directly around their waists so they are able to adjust the length of line before undertaking an ascent. Whenever it is used in this way, it must be finished off with a stopper knot.

A note of caution: Although the climber's bowline is fast to tie and easily untied, it does have a tendency to work loose, especially if the rope is stiff. It should always, therefore, be used in conjunction with a stopper knot.

Stopper knot

Use this method of tying a bowline when you need to fasten a line around an object.

Some synthetic rope might prove less reliable, so it is a good idea to secure the end with an extra half hitch, or to tuck it and trap it underneath one of the rope's strands.

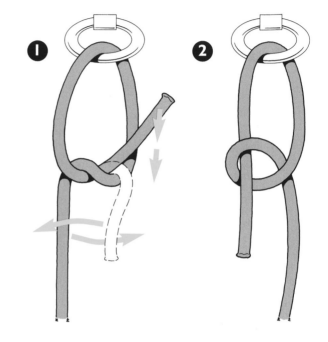

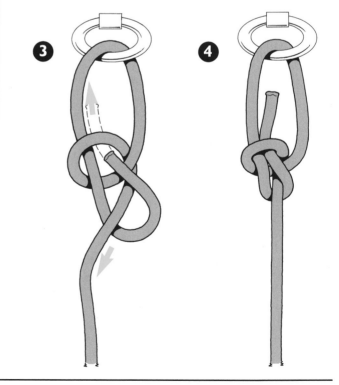

ROPE UNDER TENSION

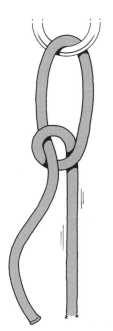

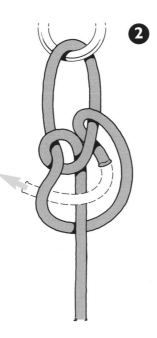

This variation for tying the bowline is particularly useful for attaching boats to rings.

The standing part stays taut throughout, while the working end is used to tie a secure fastening.

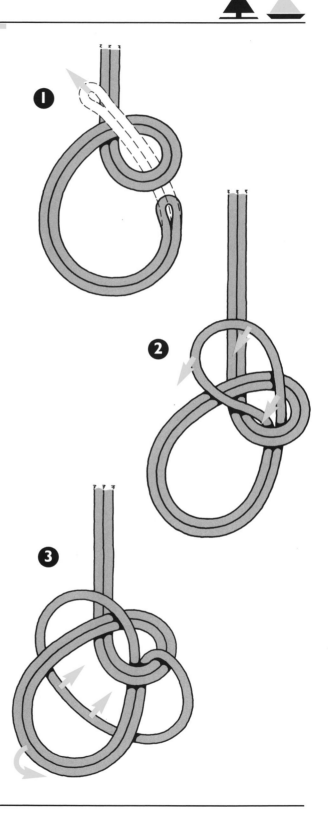

The bowline on a bight forms two fixed loops that do not slide. They are of the same diameter and overlap each other, but when opened out they can be used separately.

Although an ancient knot, it is still used today—especially in sea rescues. If the person to be rescued is conscious, he or she puts a leg through each loop and holds on to the standing part.

If the person is unconscious, both legs are put through one loop; the other loop goes under the armpits. This knot is equally effective in salvaging objects.

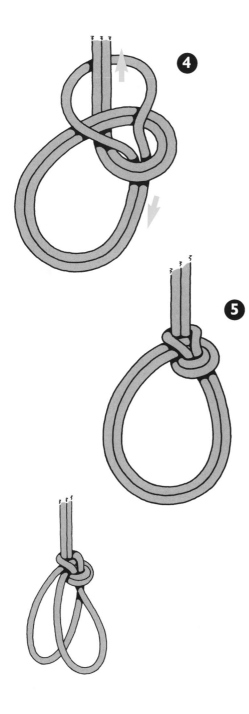

4

5

1

This sturdy, secure double-loop knot can be used as a decorative knot from which to hang gear or equipment, aboard ship or on shore.

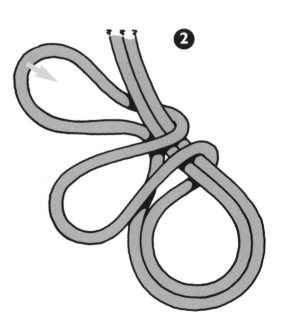

2

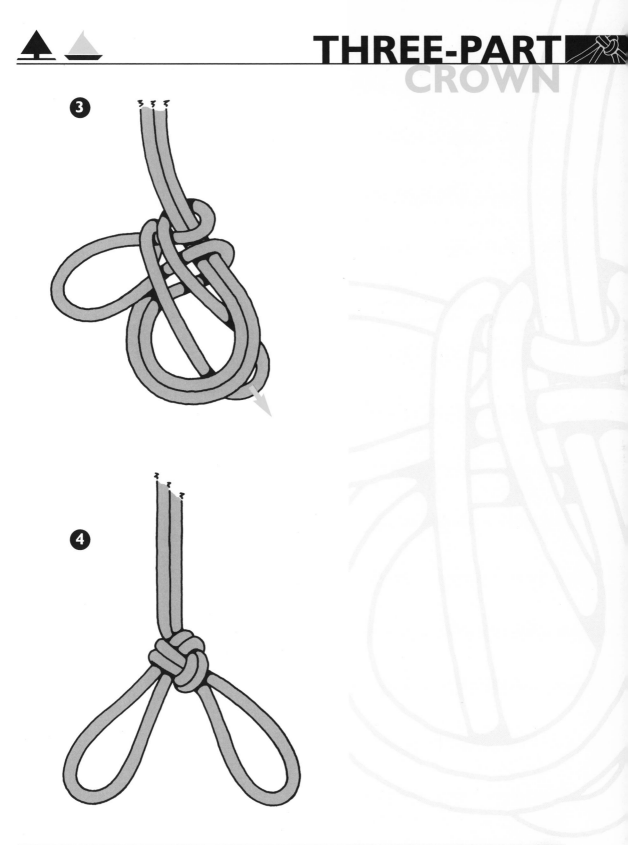

SPANISH BOWLINE

This is a very strong knot that is widely used in rescue work at sea.

The Spanish bowline can also be used to hoist large objects in a horizontal position.

Like the bowline on a bight (see page 58), it is a very old knot, formed of two separate and independent loops that will hold securely and are very safe, even under considerable strain.

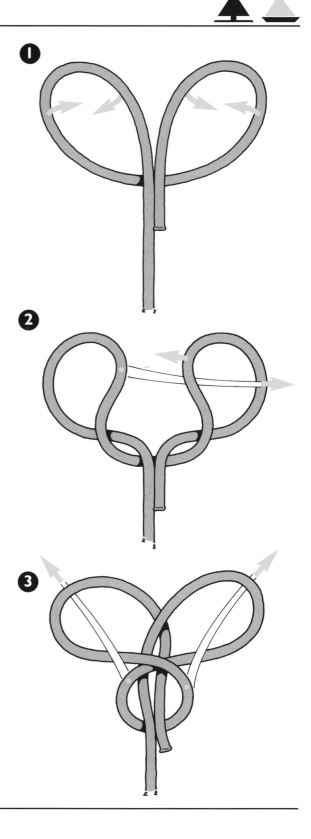

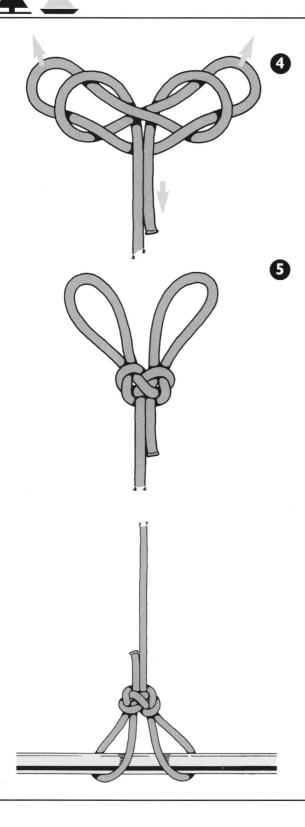

To effect a rescue, one loop is slipped over the casualty's head, around the back, and under the armpits; the other loop goes around the legs behind the knees.

It is vitally important that each loop be tightened to the individual's size and then locked into position. If this is not done properly, an unconscious casualty could easily fall through the loops.

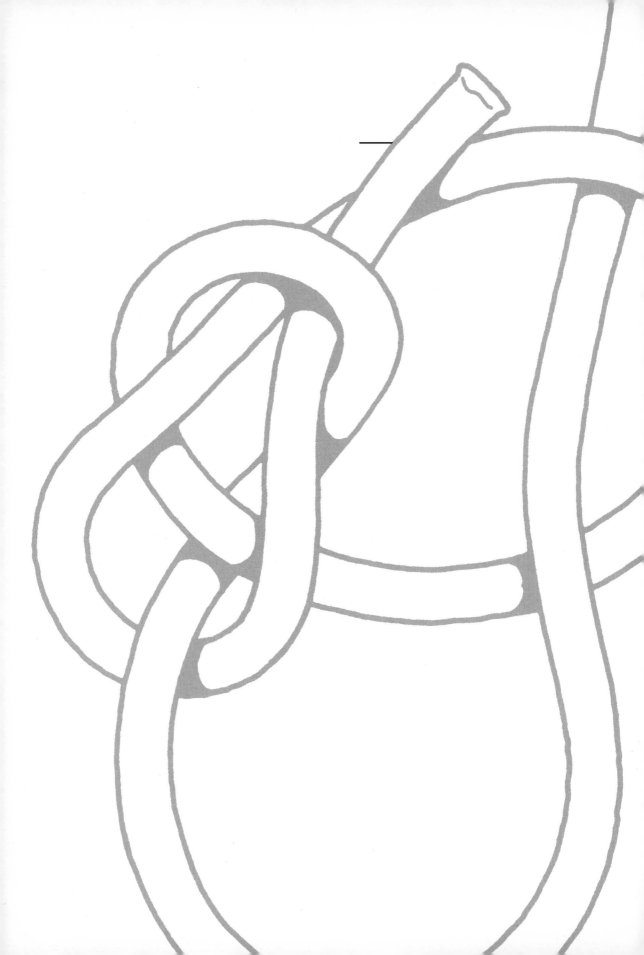

RUNNING KNOTS

Running knots, also known as slip knots or nooses, tighten around the objects on which they are tied but slacken when the strain is reduced. They are among the oldest knots known to man, having been used in prehistoric times to make weapons and trap animals. Hunters and poachers still use them today to make traps and snares. Campers and climbers use running knots to secure gear or when a rope may be subjected to heavy and sudden strain. One of the most famous, the hangman's or Jack Ketch's knot, has other, more sinister uses. They are not much used at sea, however, because of the way they slacken if not kept under constant strain.

This group of knots divides into two kinds: those formed by passing a bight through a fixed loop at the end of a line and those made from a closed bight knotted at the end of a line or along it. The main running knots in the first group are the noose and the running bowline; the hangman's knot and the tarbuck knot are the main knots in the second.

This simple knot is rarely used at sea, but it is often used by campers and hunters to snare birds and small game such as rabbits. It can also be the first knot used in tying a parcel; on a larger scale, it can be used to put tackle cables under stress.

The noose can be used as a hitch, especially if the hitch is to be formed around a very large object such as a tree trunk, because a noose can be tied using a fairly short length of line. A constrictor knot, or a clove or cow hitch, would need a much longer length of rope. Also, a noose used as a hitch is very secure.

Another useful feature of the noose is that it can be tied around relatively inaccessible objects. If you can get close enough to the object to pass a rope around it, you can tie and tighten a noose.

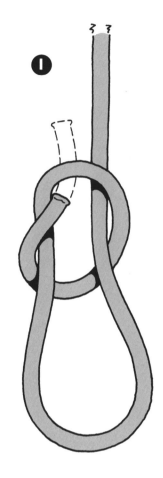

A stopper knot should be added to the noose to prevent it from slipping.

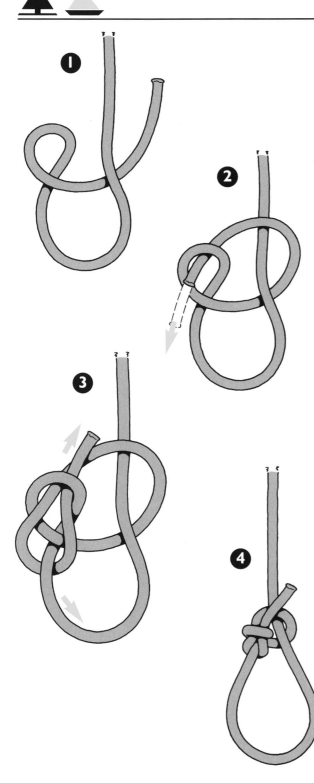

This is probably the only running knot used by sailors; it is used on running rigging and to retrieve floating objects that have fallen overboard.

On the old sailing ships this knot was used in high winds to tighten the square sail to the yardarm.

The running bowline has many uses because it is strong and secure, does not weaken rope, is simple to untie, and slides easily. It is useful for hanging objects with ropes of unequal diameters—the weight of the object creates the tension that makes the knot grip.

running knots

HANGMAN'S KNOT

This knot is one of the running knots made by knotting a closed bight at the end of the line.

It forms a very strong noose that will withstand heavy jerks and shock loading. It slides without coming undone, but not always easily, so it is usually preadjusted to the required size. The name reveals its infamous use, and the alternative name (Jack Ketch's knot) comes from the notorious hangman and executioner. Legend and superstition surround this knot; for example, its use was not permitted aboard ships of the British Royal Navy. It must always be tied with an odd number of turns, between seven and thirteen.

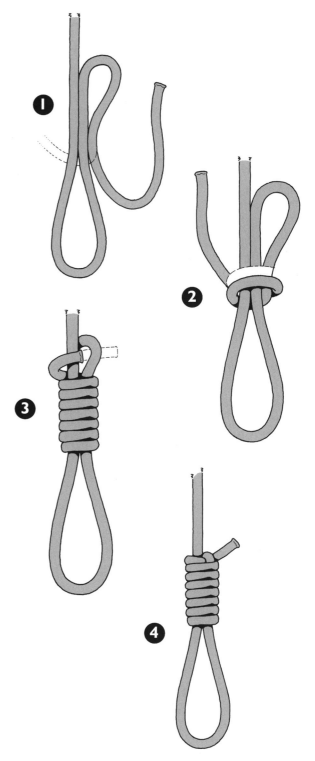

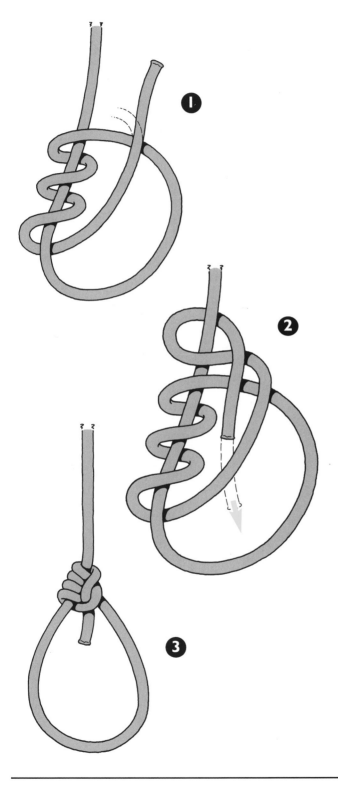

The tarbuck knot belongs to the same group of running knots as the hangman's knot; it is formed by knotting a closed bight at the end of a line.

It was developed for use by climbers when a line was likely to be subjected to heavy stress or sudden shock, because the turns made in its formation enable the knot to absorb the strain. Since the advent of double-braid (sheath-and-core) rope, it has fallen out of favor. This new rope contains its own elasticity, and the tarbuck knot's slide-and-grip action would damage the rope by stripping off the outer sheath.

It remains, however, a useful general-purpose knot, which can be slid along the standing part and grips under strain. It is not particularly secure but it can be used for improvised tent guys, as a temporary mooring for small boats, or in any other situation where lives do not directly depend upon it.

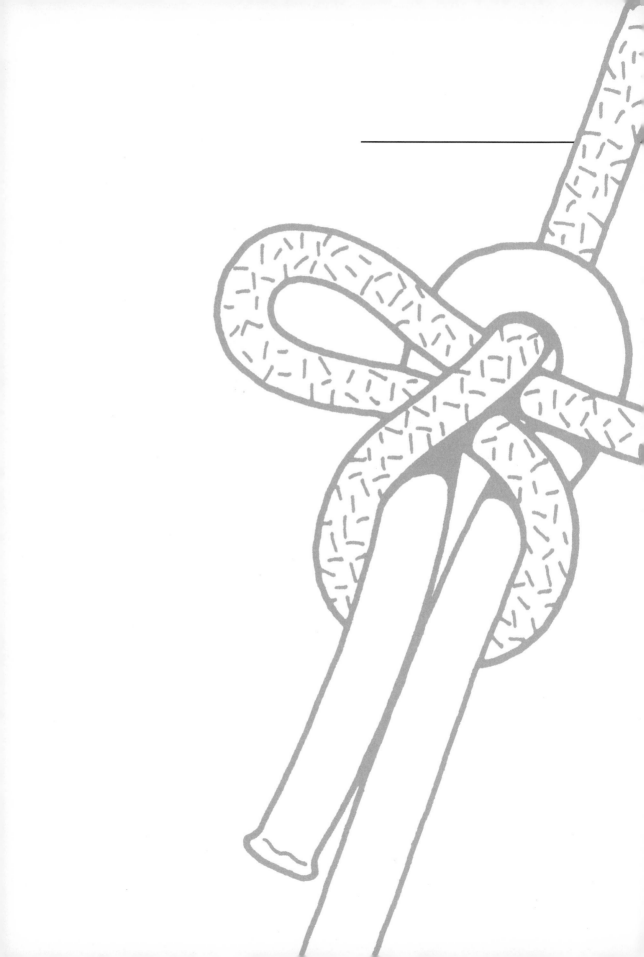

BENDS

Bends are used to join two lengths of rope at their ends to form one longer piece. It is important, if bends are to be secure, for the ropes joined in this way to be of the same kind and the same diameter. The sheet bend (see page 73) is the exception to this rule. It is secure, even when it is used to join ropes of different diameters.

Bends used at sea can often be made totally secure and more streamlined by seizing any loose ends.

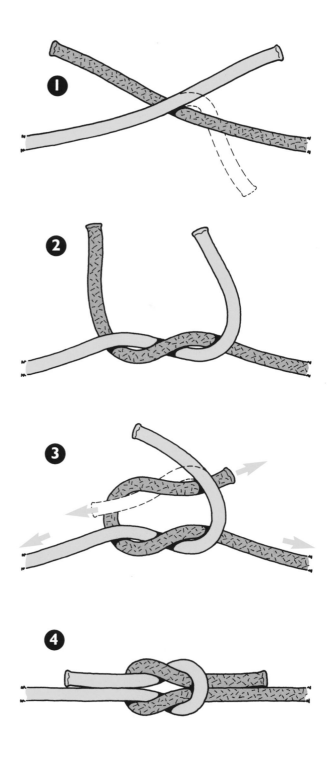

The reef knot gets its name from its nautical use: tying two ends of a rope when reefing a sail. It is often the only knot many people know, apart from the granny knot.

The reef knot is not a secure bend and should not be used as one, certainly never with ropes of different diameters. Its true function is to join together the ends of the same rope or string. It should only be used to make a temporary join in lines of identical type, weight, and diameter where it will not be put under great strain. If the lines have to take strain, you should tie stopper knots in the short ends.

The knot is made up of two half knots. The first half knot starts left over right, the second is added right over left, and both short ends finish on the same side. A correctly tied reef knot is symmetrical. If the knot is raised and uneven, it is a granny knot, which is not secure and should be avoided.

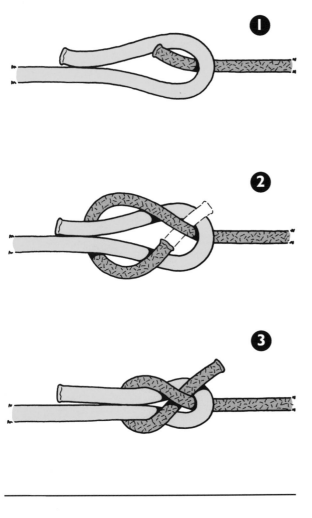

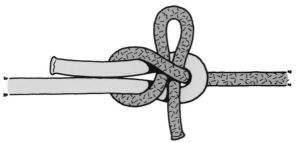

A slipped sheet bend is formed by placing a bight between the loop of the heavier rope and the standing part of the lighter one. The slipped knot is easiest to untie when the rope is under strain.

The sheet bend is probably the most commonly used of all bends, and unlike most other bends, it can safely join lines of different thicknesses.

It is not, however, 100 percent secure, especially with synthetic rope, and should never be used in circumstances where it will be subjected to great strain. Its breaking strength also decreases in direct proportion to the difference between the lines joined.

The sheet bend derives its name from the way the knot was originally used on sailing ships: to secure the ropes (known as sheets) to sails. When put to its other traditional use, as the knot used to join the corners of a flag to the rope when it is hoisted and lowered, it is known as the flag bend. It is quick to make and easy to untie (by rolling forward the bight encircling the single line), and is one of the basic knots that all sailors should know.

This knot is said to have been invented in the 19th century, but some authorities suggest it was known to the ancient Greeks.

It is generally known as the fisherman's knot, but over the years it has picked up many different names (such as angler's knot, English knot, Englishman's bend, halibut knot, true lover's knot, and waterman's knot). It is formed from two overhand knots that jam against each other; the short ends are on opposite sides and lie almost parallel to their nearest standing part. After use, the two component knots are generally easily separated and undone.

The fisherman's knot is best suited to joining thin lines such as string, cord, twine, or small stuff, and as the name suggests, it is widely used by fishermen for joining the finest of fishing lines.

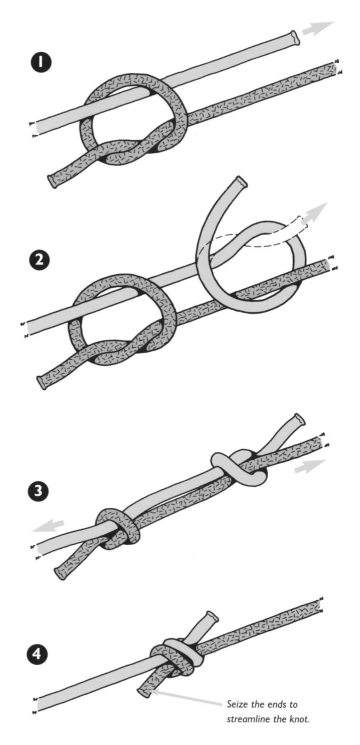

Seize the ends to streamline the knot.

▲ △ ◔ DOUBLE FISHERMAN'S KNOT

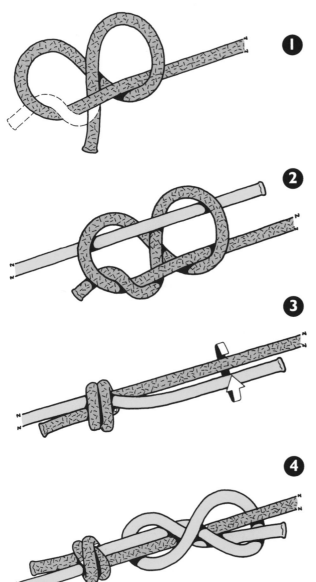

①

②

③

④

⑤

This double version of the fisherman's knot is a very strong knot for joining thin lines.

It is also known as the grapevine knot. It is quite bulky, so often the ends are seized to streamline the knot and prevent it from catching.

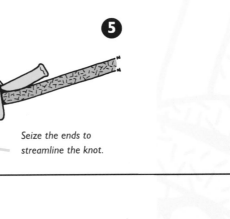

Seize the ends to streamline the knot.

bends **75**

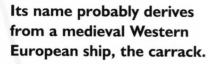

CARRICK BEND

Its name probably derives from a medieval Western European ship, the carrack.

The knot is formed from two overhand knots crossing each other. It is a very stable knot, does not slip, and is one of the most secure ways of joining two ropes of similar diameters but different types. It is rarely used as a temporary knot, as it is very hard to undo when wet or if it has been subjected to very heavy strain. It can be used with larger-diameter ropes such as hawsers, tow lines, and warp ropes.

In its flat form it is valued for its distinctive symmetrical appearance and has long been a favorite among artists and graphic designers. When it is drawn up it capsizes into an entirely different shape, but this has no detrimental effect on its strength or security.

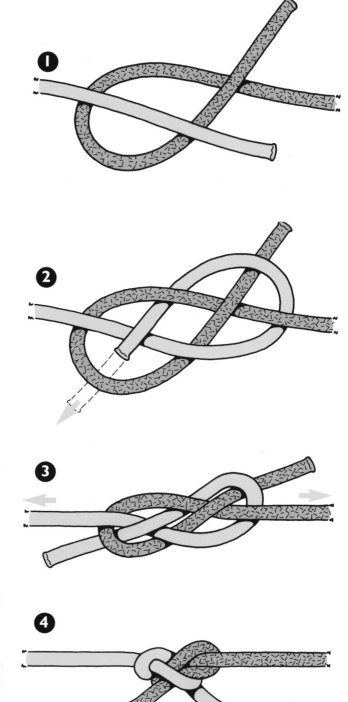

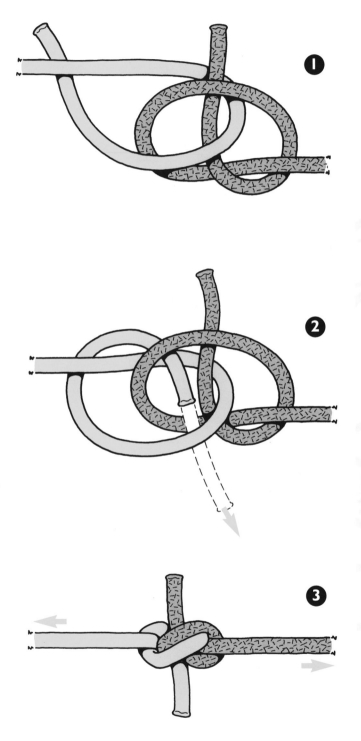

The Hunter's bend or rigger's bend is based on two overhand knots.

It is stable, has good grip, and is stronger than the sheet bend or the reef knot. It also has the advantage of being easy to untie.

The name Hunter's bend came from Dr. Edward Hunter, a retired physician, who was reported to have invented the knot in 1968. Subsequent research, however, revealed his knot to be the same as the rigger's bend described nearly 20 years earlier by Phil D. Smith in a book called *Knots for Mountaineers*. He had devised the knot while working on the waterfront in San Francisco. Whoever first invented it, the Hunter's bend or the rigger's bend remains a good general-purpose sailing knot with many useful qualities.

SURGEON'S KNOT

This knot, as the name suggests, is used by surgeons to suture wounds and tie off blood vessels.

It is also an excellent sailing knot for joining two lengths of rope or line together. It is less bulky than other knots and has a good grip. It twists as it is drawn up tight and the diagonal is wrapped around it.

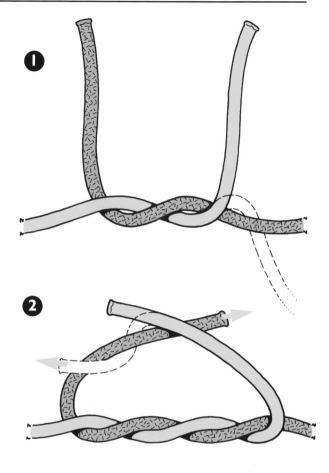

bends

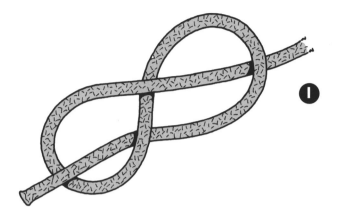

1

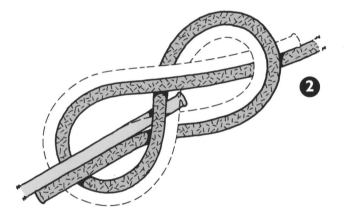

This simple knot (also known as the Flemish bend or knot) is tied by making a figure-eight knot in one end of a line and then following it around with the other working end.

It is, despite its simplicity, one of the strongest bends and holds equally well in string and rope.

2

3

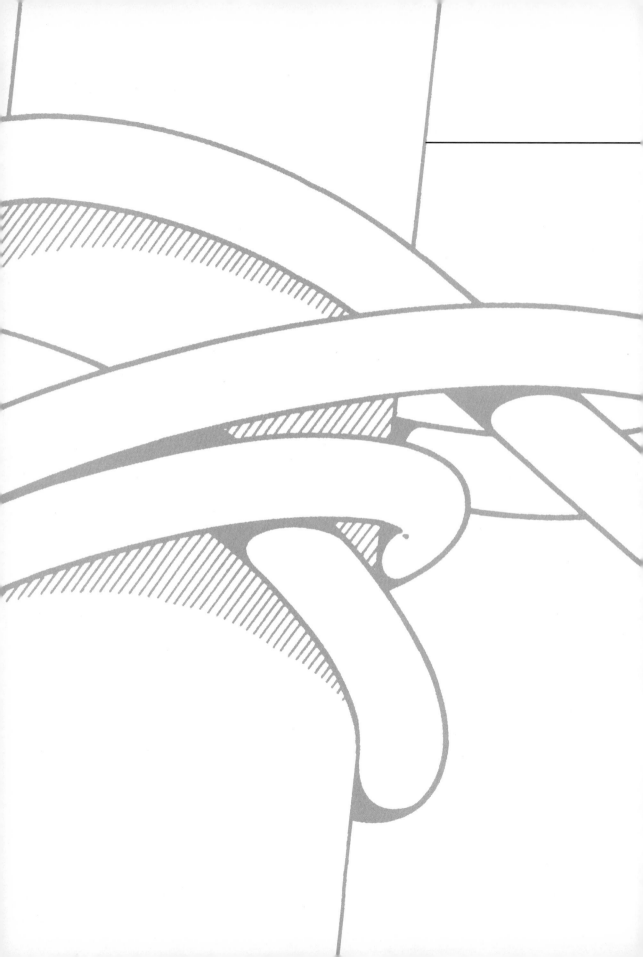

HITCHES

Hitches are knots used to secure a rope to another object (such as a post, hook, spar, or rail), or to another rope that does not play any part in the actual tying.

They are widely used in sailing for mooring boats, fastening lines, and lashing. They can stand parallel strain without slipping and have the advantage of being very quick to tie once learned.

HALF
HITCHES

The half hitch is a very widely used fastening. It is, in fact, a single hitch formed around the standing part of another hitch.

It is used to complete and strengthen other knots—such as the round turn and two half hitches (see page 92)—which can then be used for tying, hanging, or hooking objects. The slipped half hitch is a useful variation of the simple half hitch; a sharp pull on the end releases the knot.

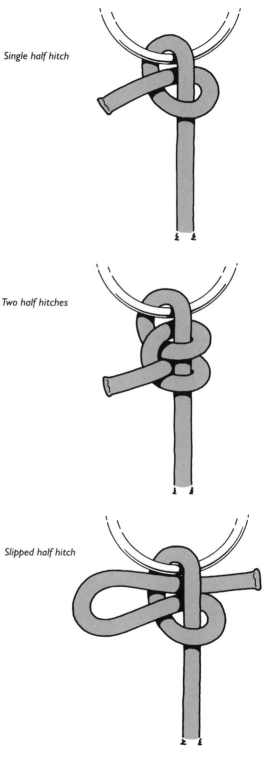

Single half hitch

Two half hitches

Slipped half hitch

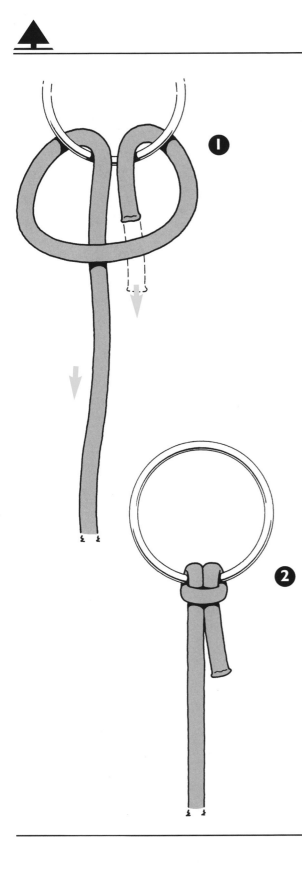

This hitch, also known as the lanyard hitch, is composed of two single hitches and is usually made on a ring or post.

Often used for tethering animals, it is the least secure of all the hitches and should only be used as a temporary fastening.

This hitch is specifically used for attaching buntlines to the eyes or eyelet holes on sails.

The buntline hitch needs to be very secure so as to avoid loosening in the strong winds that constantly buffet sails. Its strength comes from the short end being deliberately trapped inside the knot.

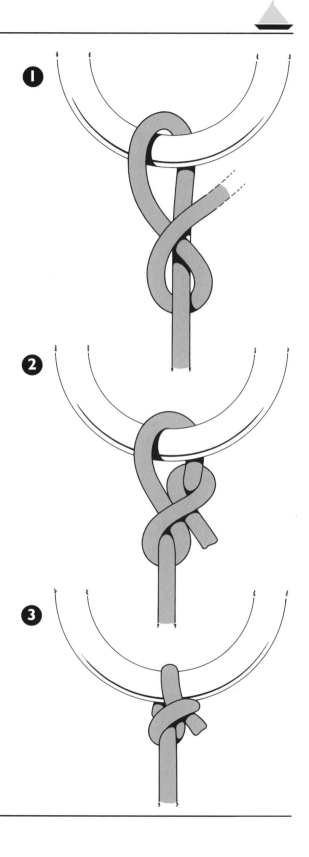

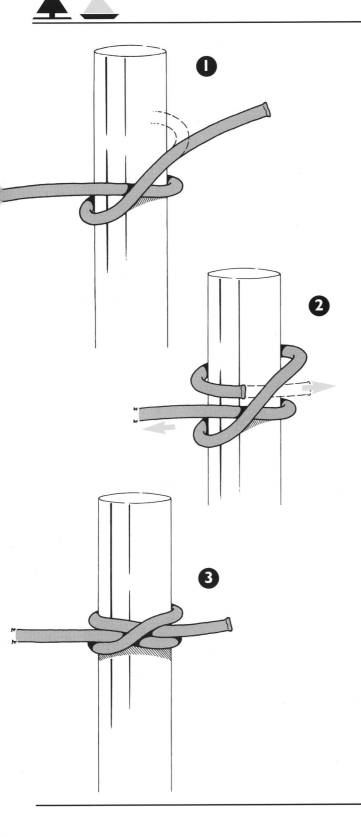

The clove hitch is one of the best known and most valuable of hitches, and is used extensively on most yachts.

It can be used to fasten a line to a rail, post, or bollard, or onto another rope that is not part of the knot. It can, with practice, be tied with one hand. As one of its other names, the boatman's knot, suggests, it is particularly useful for sailors who may need to moor a dinghy to a dock with one hand while holding on to a rail with the other.

The clove hitch is not, however, a totally secure mooring knot; it will work loose if strain is intermittent and comes from different angles. It is best used as a temporary hold, and then replaced by a more stable knot. It can be made more secure by adding one or two half hitches around the standing part of the rope, or by adding a stopper knot.

CLOVE HITCH

OVER A POST

This knot is formed by dropping two overlapping half hitches over a post.

It is widely used in sailing for mooring boats to posts or pilings at docks. It is also used by campers to tighten guy ropes.

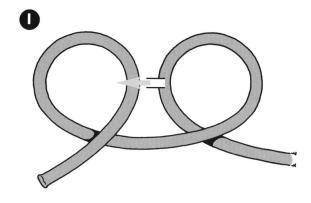

❶

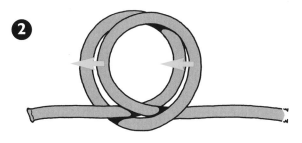

❷

❸

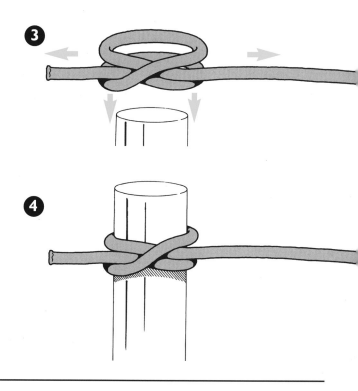

❹

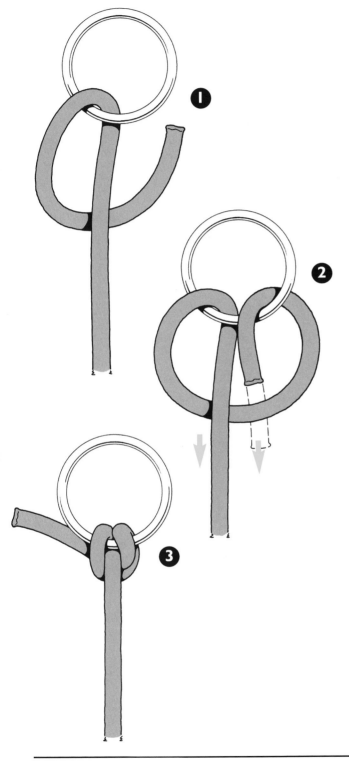

This version is commonly used in climbing and mountaineering.

It can regulate the length of rope between the climber and the piton (a spike driven into the rock or crack to support the rope). In sailing, where the ring is usually finer than the rope, the constant strain on the rope would cause dangerous chafing.

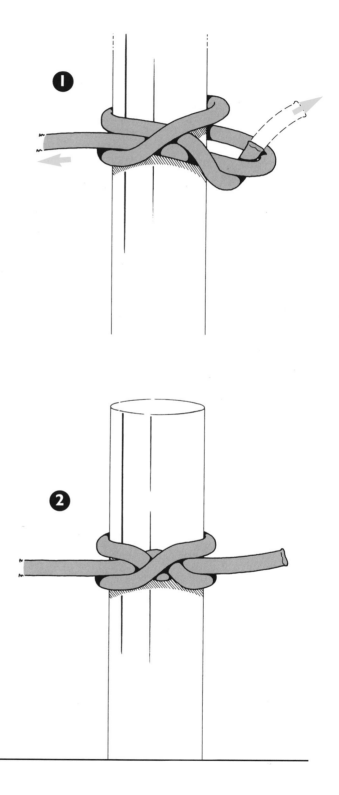

This is a popular all-purpose knot because it is firm and does not slip.

It is particularly useful for creating a quick temporary whipping on the ends of ropes.

The knot is made by taking two turns with the rope, and forming an overhand knot in the second. The left end is then threaded under the first turn, trapping the overhand knot under a crosswise turn that holds it firmly in place. The constrictor knot grips firmly and stays tied. It may have to be cut free unless the last tuck is made with a bight to make a slip knot.

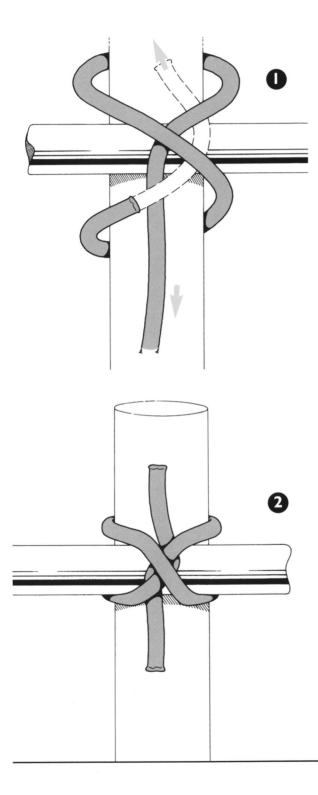

①

This is similar to a constrictor knot. It is used to fix together crossed pieces of rigid material and has a wide range of sailing uses; for example, to secure paddles to luggage racks.

If used as a permanent knot, the ends may be trimmed off for neatness.

②

The pile hitch is a very neat and practical hitch for securing objects to a post.

It is ideal for a temporary mooring of a boat. The big advantage of this hitch is that it is very easy to tie quickly.

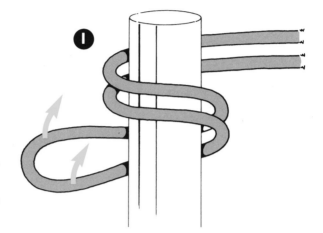

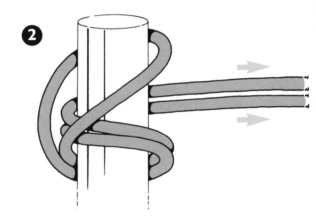

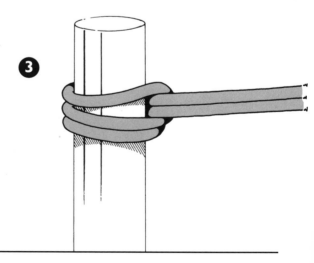

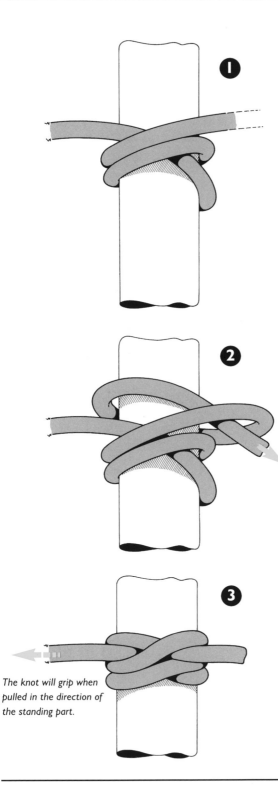

This is an essential knot for sailboarders. It is derived from the clove hitch but is significantly more secure.

It is used on sailboards to secure the wishbone boom to the mast, but can equally well be used to make any line fast to other cylindrical objects. This very effective, reliable knot is easy to tie and grips itself, but only in one direction.

The knot will grip when pulled in the direction of the standing part.

ROUND TURN AND
TWO HALF HITCHES

This knot is strong, dependable, and never jams. This makes it a very versatile sailing knot; you can use it whenever you want to fasten a line to a ring, post, bollard, deck eye, rail, or beam.

It moors boats safely and will support heavy loads. It has another advantage in that once one end has been secured with a round turn and two half hitches, the other end can be tied with a second knot. This is especially useful when fastening unwieldy, bulky objects.

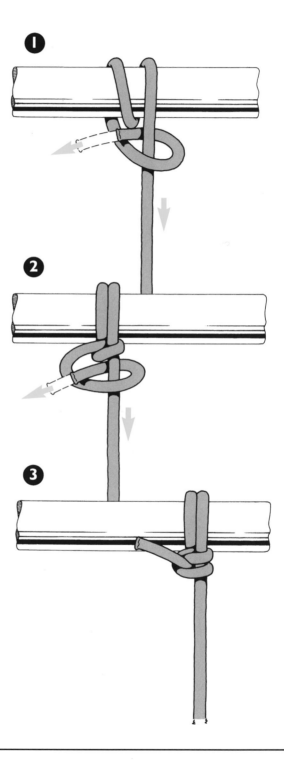

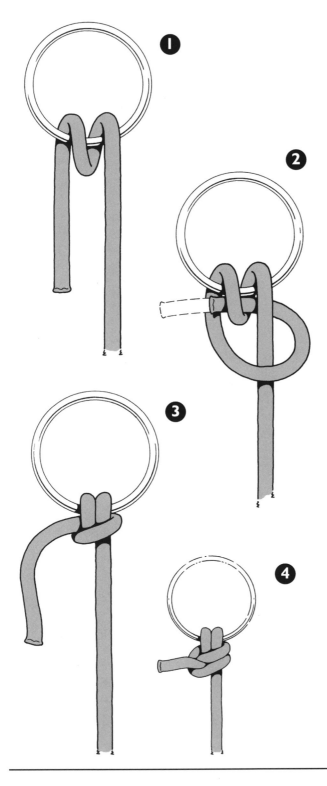

The fisherman's bend is one of the most secure and widely used hitches.

It is formed by making two turns around the post or through the ring and then tucking the working end through both turns. Adding a half hitch makes it extra secure.

It is used by sailors, to whom it is known as the anchor bend, to secure boats at the dock; it can also tie onto an anchor ring. If it is used in this way, you should add a stopper knot for safety.

The name of this knot comes from its legendary use by highwaymen and robbers to give them quick release of their horses' reins and so ensure a fast getaway. It is also called the draw hitch.

One pull on the working end and the knot is undone, but the standing end can be put under tension. It is useful for tethering animals, for lowering loads, and as a temporary fastening.

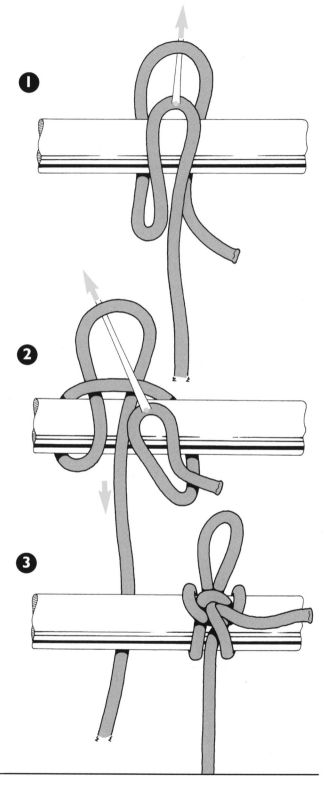

❶

❷

❸

WAGGONER'S HITCH

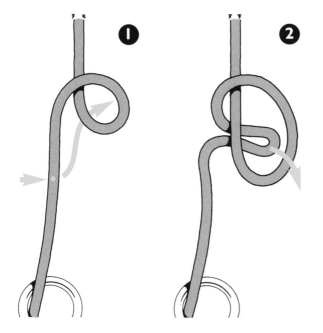

The waggoner's hitch is a very useful, practical knot that makes it possible to pull tight a line or rope yet leave it ready for immediate release.

This makes it an ideal knot for securing loads or deck gear. Once the line has been heaved tight, it should be secured with at least two half hitches.

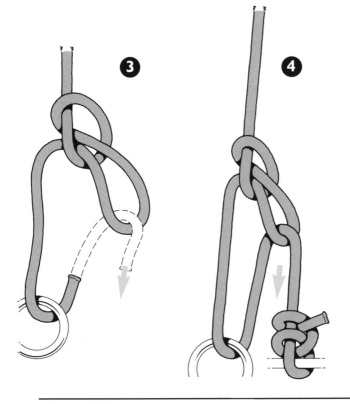

hitches 95

PRUSIK
KNOT

This knot was devised by Dr.
Carl Prusik in 1931. It is
used by climbers to attach
slings to rope in such a way
that they slide freely when
the knot is loose but hold
firm under a sideways load.

It is used as a safety mechanism
in abseiling and rappelling
(descending a steep rock face
by using a doubled rope fixed at
a higher point). The Prusik knot
is useful for anyone who has to
scale awkward heights—for
example, tree surgeons and
cavers—as well as rock
climbers.

The Prusik knot does not
always slide easily, and once
the load is in place, it can only
be released by removing the
weight and freeing the turns of
the rope. The knot must be tied
with rope that is considerably
thinner than the line to which it
is tied, and it is important to
remember that it can slip if the
rope is wet or icy.

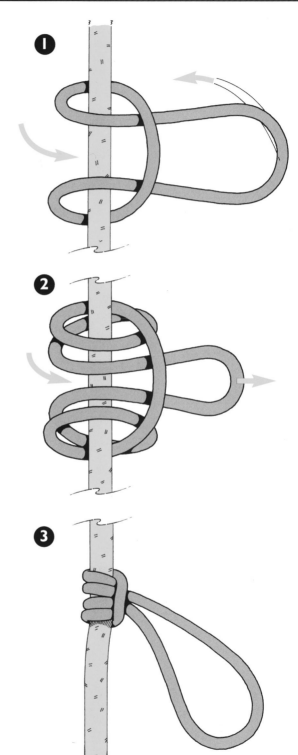

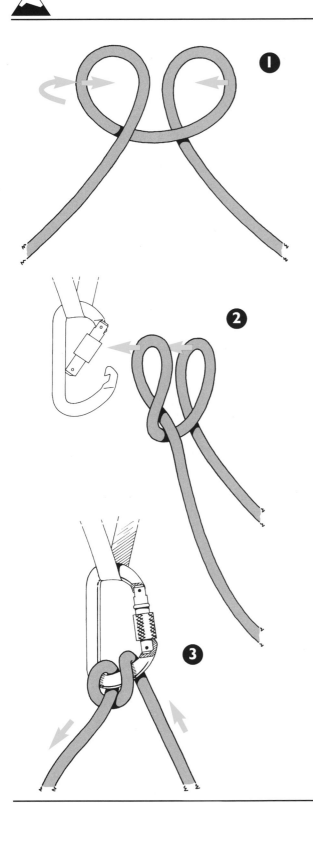

1

2

3

The Italian hitch is an innovative climbing knot used for belaying, and was introduced into the mountaineers' lexicon of knots in 1974. Its chief advantage lies in the way it absorbs the energy of a fall.

The rope is passed around and through a carabiner and will check the climber's fall by locking up. The climbing rope can also be paid out or pulled in to provide slack or tension when required.

It is the official means of belaying (that is, fixing a running rope around a rock or cleat) of the Union Internationale des Associations d'Alpinisme. The major disadvantage of this knot, also called the munter friction hitch or sliding ring hitch, is that it is easy to tie incorrectly.

This hitch can be tied with large-diameter rope and is useful when a knot has to be made and untied quickly.

It is not commonly used in sailing; it's associated more with camping activities. It is useful for hoisting light objects.

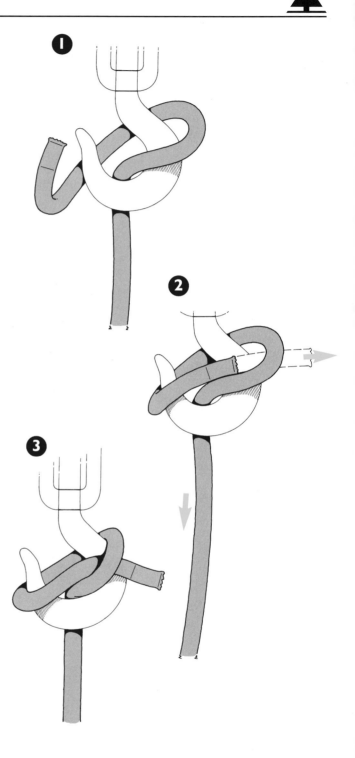

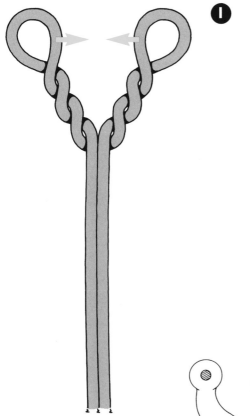

This is the best hook knot for rope of medium diameter because the strain is equal on both sides.

It has a long history of use on the docks and at sea for lifting and slinging heavy loads. This very secure knot can be used, for example, on the hook of a crane in the marina.

 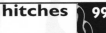

The timber hitch is a temporary noose formed around such objects as tree trunks, planks, and poles so that they can be dragged, pulled, raised, or lowered.

It is made by doubling the working end on itself and twisting it around its own part (not the standing part of the hitch) several times. If the object is very thick, more twists are added. It is a very useful hitch in that it can be quickly put on, is very secure, and does not jam. Unfortunately, it is easy for beginners to tie it incorrectly.

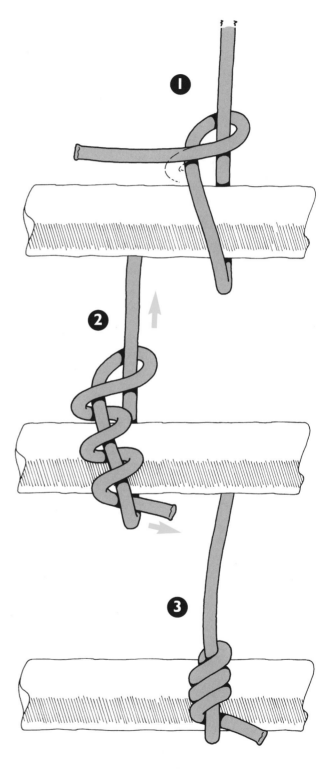

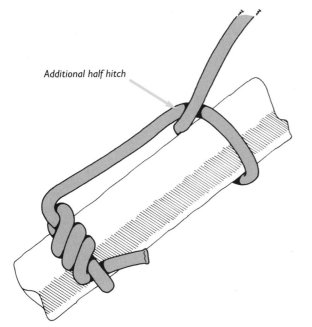

Additional half hitch

The killick hitch is a variation of the timber hitch specifically used for dragging and towing.

It is created by first tying a timber hitch and then, some distance down the line, adding a half hitch.

CLEATING
A LINE

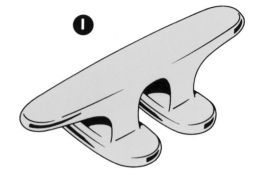

A cleat is a deck fitting to which lines are tied on a temporary basis. The line is made fast to the cleat with a hitch. This particular hitch is often the first knot that prospective sailors come into contact with.

It is a simple but effective hitch, but it is also a hitch that many people tie incorrectly. It is easy to think that the more turns you put around a cleat, the stronger the connection is going to be. This is not correct. If tied correctly, this hitch only requires a couple of turns to grip firmly; this also makes it quicker to release.

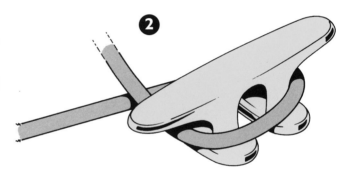

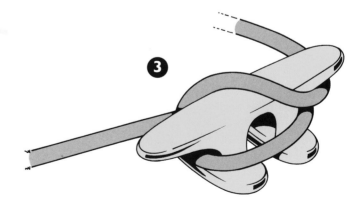

4

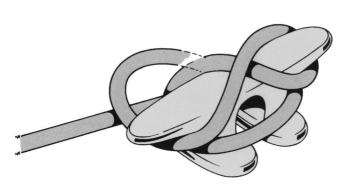

Because lines have to be alternately made fast and quickly released as a matter of course in sailing, this is an important knot to learn.

5

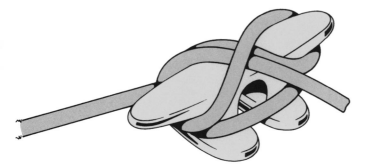

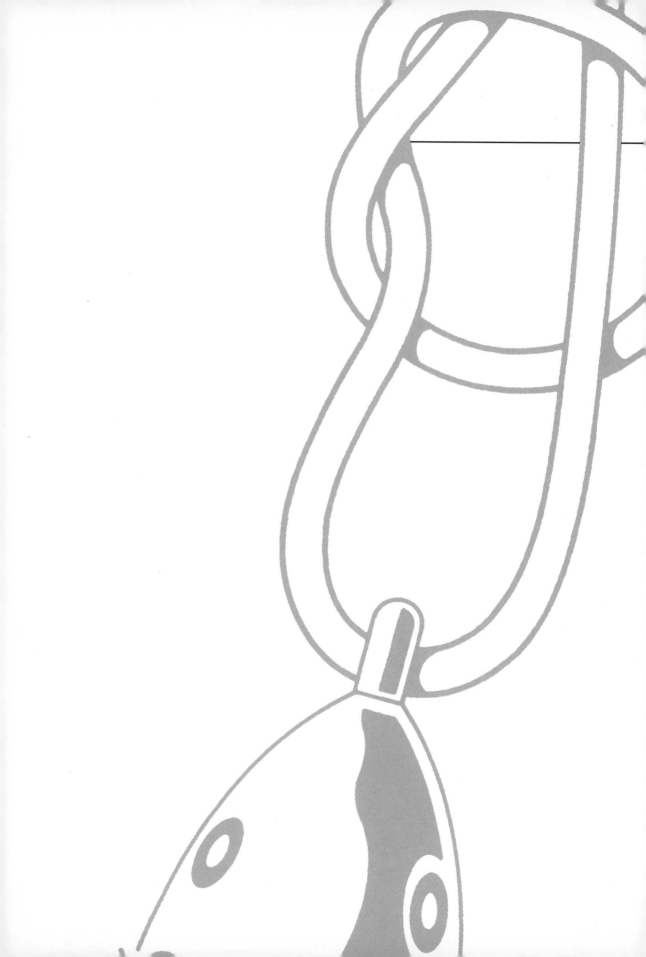

FISHING
KNOTS

Any fishing knot is a vital link in a tackle system. If that knot is faulty or incorrectly tied, it becomes the weak link of the system—and it is always the weak link that snaps first. This demonstrates how important knots are to the fisherman.

Here are a few tips that are specific to tying effective fishing knots:

- Before tying any knot, always check your line for any visible signs of damage. If in doubt, safely discard that section of the line.

- To reduce friction and to help the knot seat correctly, lubricate it with saliva or water before drawing it together.

- Once the knot has been tightened as much as possible and seated correctly, trim the knot ends to avoid them catching on rod rings, hooks, or weeds.

- Visually check your knot—good knots look good. If you are not fully confident that the knot has been tied and seated correctly—don't gamble!

This chapter does not aim to cover every fishing knot invented, but it does look in detail at the knots that have been tried and tested by generations of fishermen. Because of the wide variations of type and manufacture in available fishing lines, the suggested number of turns are only recommendations; a certain amount of experimentation may be required. If your fishing knot is tied correctly and you are fully confident with it, you have eliminated the most vulnerable weak link in your tackle system.

KNOTS FOR
JOINING
LINES

The joining of two lines is one of the most important connections in a tackle system.

The four tested and reliable knots in this section, when correctly tied, will provide secure connections. Because of the wide variety of line materials and sizes available, the number of turns required in each knot will differ. A general guideline is given, but a certain amount of experimentation may be required for you to achieve the optimum number of turns.

1

The Albright knot is one of the most effective fishing knots for joining lines of different materials and unequal diameters—for example, when tying backing line to a fly line or monofilament lines of widely different sizes.

Make at least 12 turns.

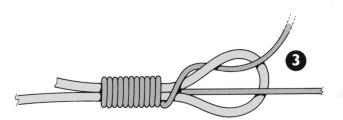

2

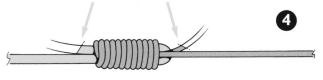

3

Trim the knot ends.

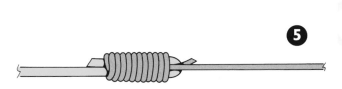

4

5

This knot is a firm favorite with many fishermen and one of the most widely used fishing knots in the world.

It has a relatively high knot strength, with the turns (a minimum of five with each line) helping it absorb strain and shock. It is most effective for joining monofilament lines of the same or similar diameters, but can also be used in many other fishing situations.

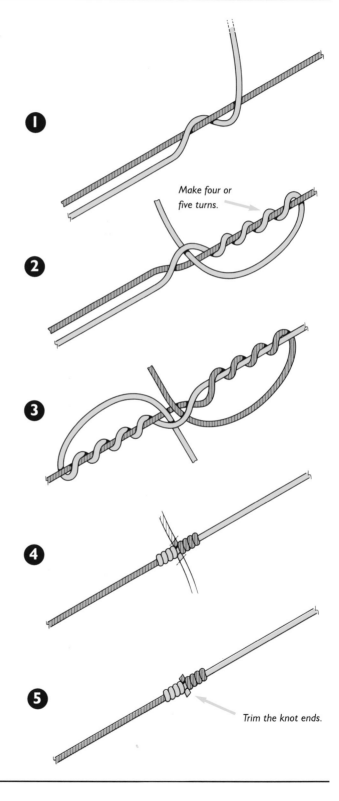

1

2 *Make four or five turns.*

3

4

5 *Trim the knot ends.*

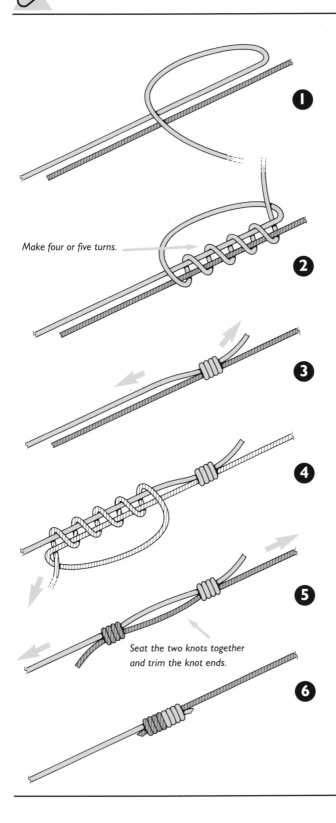

①

②

Make four or five turns.

③

④

⑤

Seat the two knots together and trim the knot ends.

⑥

The double uni-knot, also known as the double grinner knot, is a pair of uni- or grinner knots tied back to back with the two knots seating against each other and forming a very strong connection.

It is an easy knot to tie and is one of the most effective ways of joining two sections of a tippet or leader.

❶

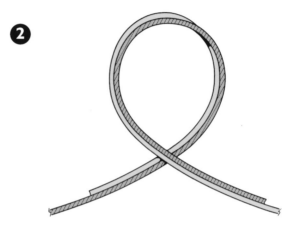

Also known as the surgeon's knot, this very efficient knot is a true all-arounder.

It is fast to tie and it can be used with lines of equal or unequal diameters as well as differing materials. To properly construct this knot, one of the lines must be short enough to enable the end to pass through the loop.

❷

❸

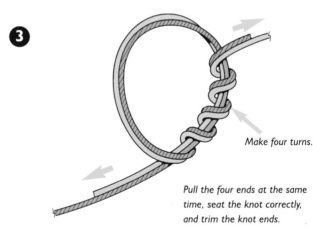

Make four turns.

Pull the four ends at the same time, seat the knot correctly, and trim the knot ends.

❹

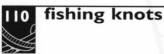

FISHING
LOOPS

Correctly tied loops are exceptionally strong, and for many anglers the interlocking-loop system (see page 112) is an integral part of the tackle system.

Loops have a wide range of fishing applications, and the interlocking-loop system provides the perfect answer for any line connection that needs to be changed frequently. A good example is being able to change a premade leader quickly and efficiently while fishing. Because no actual knot tying is involved, this can be a real advantage in adverse weather conditions or poor light.

The surgeon's or double loop is a quick and successful loop that does not slip when tied properly.

It is tied in exactly the same way as the surgeon's knot (see page 78), except it is constructed from a single length of line.

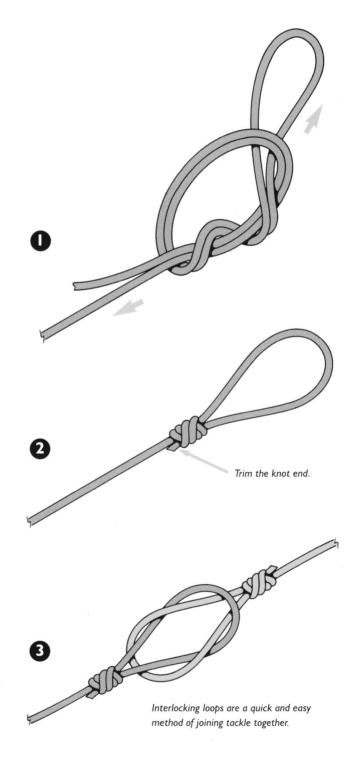

1

2

Trim the knot end.

3

Interlocking loops are a quick and easy method of joining tackle together.

1

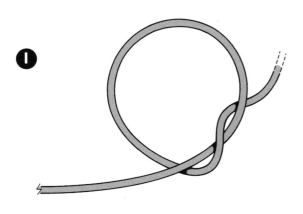

This knot, also known as the blood loop, forms a right-angled loop in the line.

It is an excellent way for fly fishermen to attach additional flies (called droppers) to the line. It can also be used to attach weights and extra hooks to create a paternoster system (a weighted line with a series of hooks positioned at intervals along it) for boat and beach fishing.

2

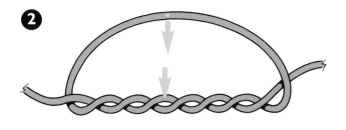

3

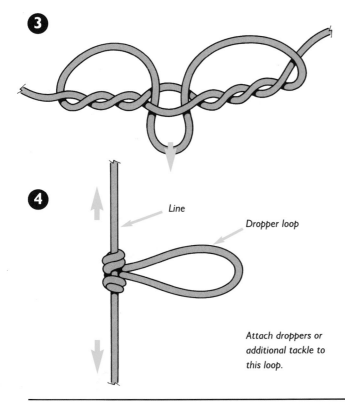

4

Line

Dropper loop

Attach droppers or
additional tackle to
this loop.

The Bimini twist provides 100 percent knot strength, making it one of the most secure loops possible.

Originally developed for big-game fishing, it can be tied in monofilament or braided line and used with both light and heavy tackle. This knot may take a little time to master, but its strength will prove invaluable in any line-connection system.

❶

❷

Form an initial loop around a solid object before starting to make the turns.

Depending on the type of line being used, make between 8 and 20 turns in this direction. For regular monofilament, 15 turns are recommended.

Keep the turns
firm and tight.

3

Make approximately
the same number of turns
back in this direction.

4

5

Remove the loop
from the solid object.

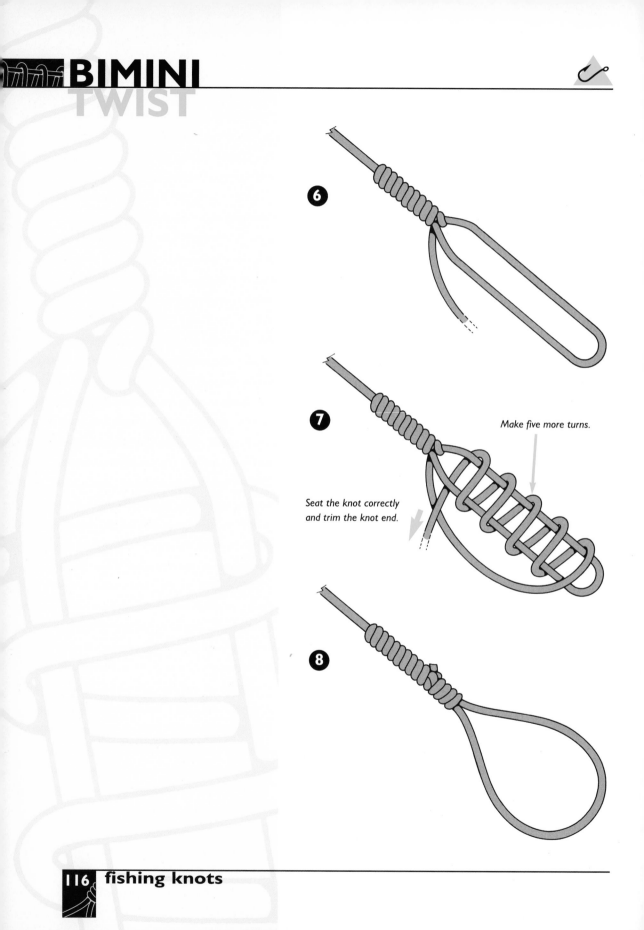

6

7

Make five more turns.

Seat the knot correctly
and trim the knot end.

8

JOINING
LINE TO A
FLY LINE

A fly line requires a secure knot at both ends—to attach the backing line at one end, and to attach the butt section of the leader at the other.

This section covers various methods of tying these knots, some of which can initially prove difficult. Follow the instructions closely and practice before tying the final knot. If you are not totally confident with your knots, seek help from your local tackle store. In most cases, the owner will be only too pleased to help out.

NAIL KNOT

The main use for this knot is to attach backing line to a fly line.

To tie the knot you need a small-diameter nail—hence the name—but a straightened paper clip or needle will do the job just as well. The nail acts to stiffen the fly line while forming the knot, and then to provide a passage through which to return the line.

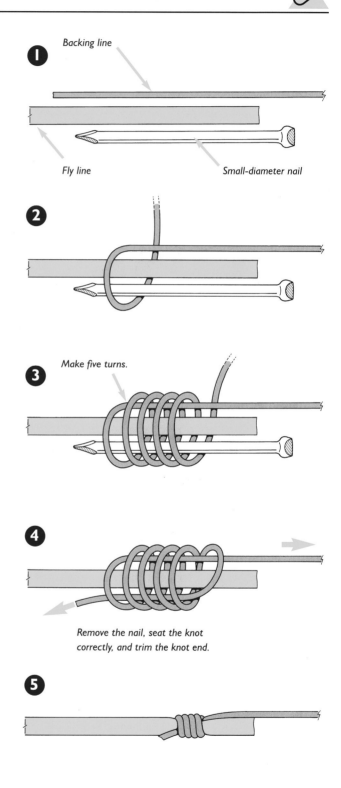

1

Backing line

Fly line   Small-diameter nail

2

3 Make five turns.

4

Remove the nail, seat the knot correctly, and trim the knot end.

5

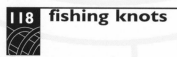

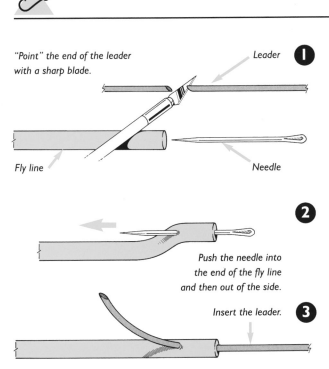

"Point" the end of the leader with a sharp blade.

Leader **1**

Fly line

Needle

This knot is used specifically to create an extremely strong and streamlined connection between the fly line and the monofilament leader.

Correctly tied, it will not catch or snag on the rod rings when you play a fish.

2

Push the needle into the end of the fly line and then out of the side.

Insert the leader. **3**

Should it prove difficult to insert the leader, replace the needle, heat the needle point, and then remove. This will keep the hole open, but be careful not to damage the lines with any excess heat.

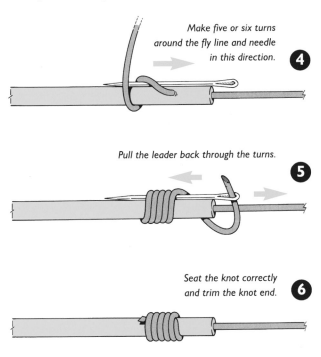

Make five or six turns around the fly line and needle in this direction. **4**

Pull the leader back through the turns.

5

Seat the knot correctly and trim the knot end. **6**

NEEDLE

MONO LOOP

If you change your leader on a regular basis, then as an alternative to attaching a single line leader to your fly line, you can create a mono loop with which to attach your leader by using the quick and easy interlocking-loop method.

The tying method is the same as for the needle knot (see page 119), except you are using a double line instead of a single one.

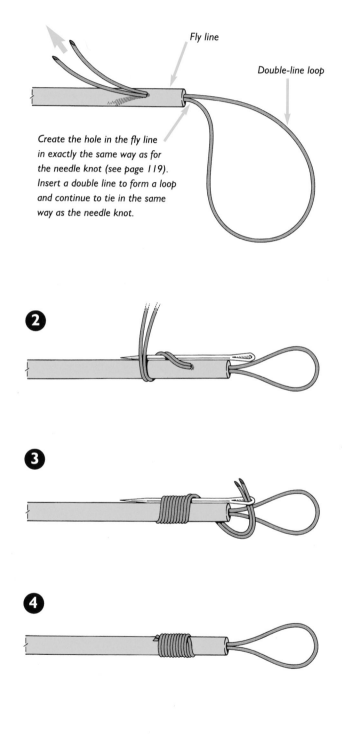

1

Fly line

Double-line loop

Create the hole in the fly line in exactly the same way as for the needle knot (see page 119). Insert a double line to form a loop and continue to tie in the same way as the needle knot.

2

3

4

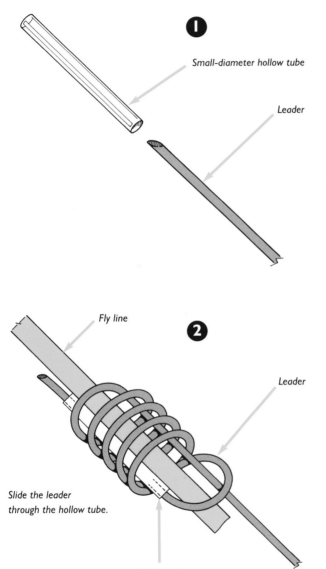

1

Small-diameter hollow tube

Leader

The tying method for both the nail knot (see page 118) and the needle knot (see page 119) can be greatly improved by substituting a small-diameter hollow tube for the traditional nail or needle.

2

Fly line

Leader

Slide the leader through the hollow tube.

Hollow tube

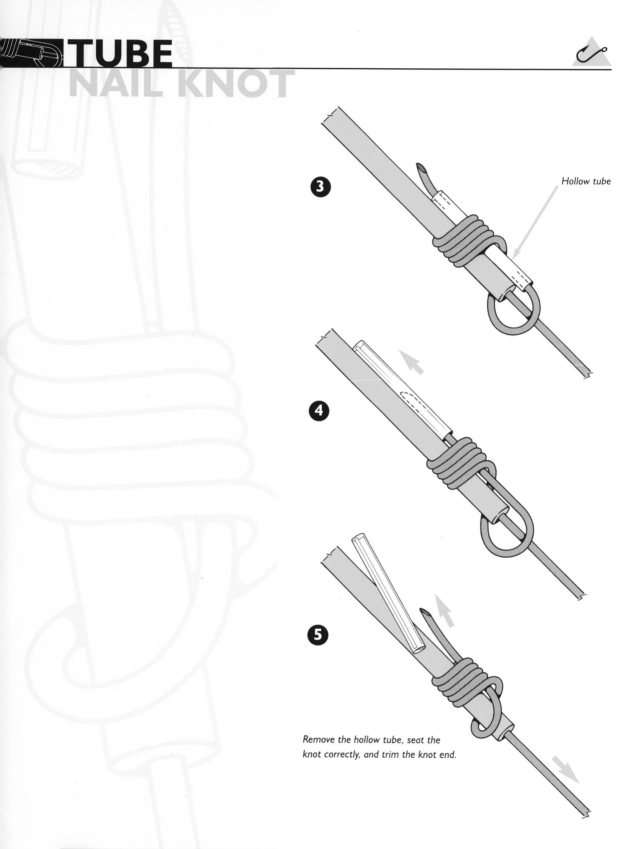

3

Hollow tube

4

5

Remove the hollow tube, seat the
knot correctly, and trim the knot end.

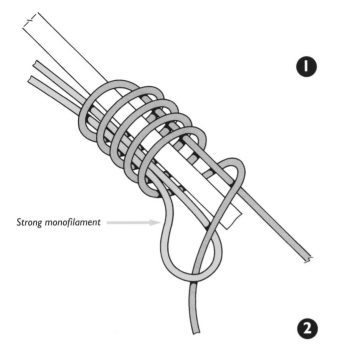

1

If you find yourself in an emergency, needing to tie a nail knot to attach backing or a leader to a fly line and not having a nail or needle, you can create an emergency knot using a piece of strong monofilament.

Strong monofilament

2

Pull the leader through using the monofilament, and finish the knot in the same way as the nail knot (see page 118).

KNOTS FOR
HOOKS
AND TACKLE

The knots in this section are for attaching hooks and flies to a leader or tippet, and attaching various items of tackle—lures, swivels, and sinkers—to a line.

An important aspect of choosing which knot to use is to feel fully confident with that knot. The knot you eventually choose will be a vital link between you and your quarry, so practice and experiment with it until you feel confident.

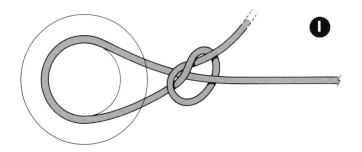

1

The first and most basic connection the fisherman needs is to secure one end of the line to the reel or spool.

The arbor knot or reel knot is easy to tie and has proved to be an effective knot for this purpose.

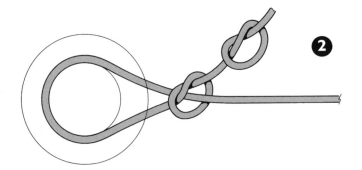

2

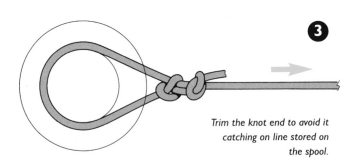

3

Trim the knot end to avoid it catching on line stored on the spool.

1

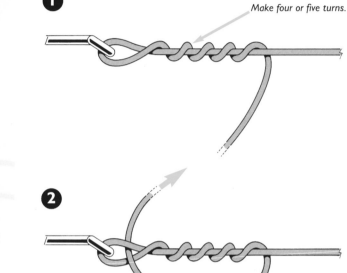

Make four or five turns.

Also known as the tucked half blood knot, this old, tried-and-tested knot is a firm favorite with many fishermen.

It is very successfully tied with fine monofilament, but when heavier monofilament is used it can prove difficult to draw the knot up tightly.

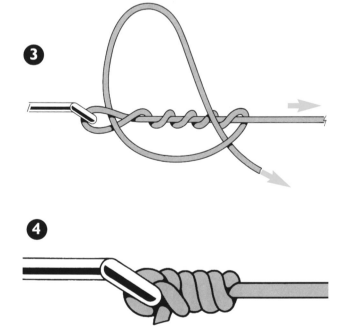

2

3

4

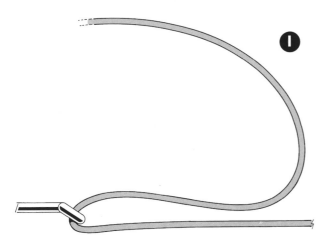

Also known as the grinner knot, this is an extremely reliable knot for attaching eyed hooks, swivels, and sinkers.

It can be used with most types and sizes of line.

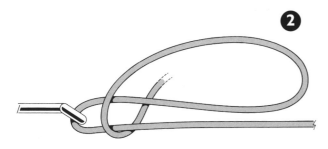

Make four or five turns.

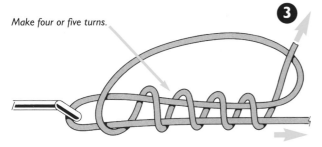

Seat the knot correctly and trim the knot end.

This simple and effective knot is best used with swivels, lures, or large-eyed hooks.

It can draw up into a rather bulky knot, so it is not suitable for use with very light tackle.

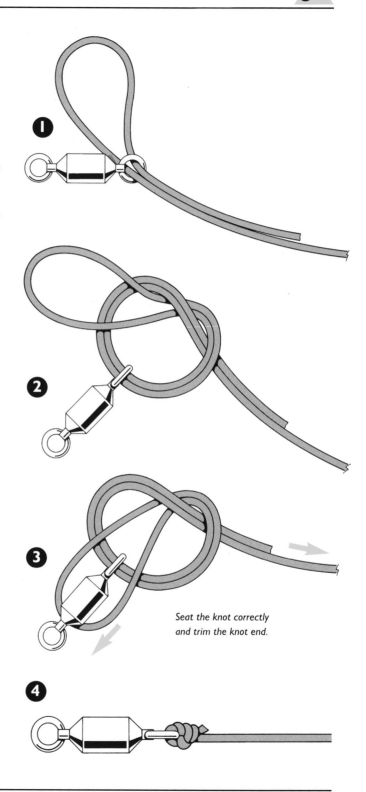

Seat the knot correctly
and trim the knot end.

❶

❷

Make four turns.

❸

Seat the knot correctly and trim the knot end.

❹

The nonslip knot and the loop it creates will give the lure a better action in the water.

An artificial lure attached with a loop and knotted with this nonslip knot will move around more in the water, creating a better action—whereas a tightly seated knot will restrict the lure's movement.

This knot has proved successful with both light and heavy tackle.

IMPROVED
TURLE KNOT

Exclusively for flies on hooks with upturned or downturned eyes, this simple but strong knot will keep the head of the fly in line with the cast, giving a more effective fly presentation.

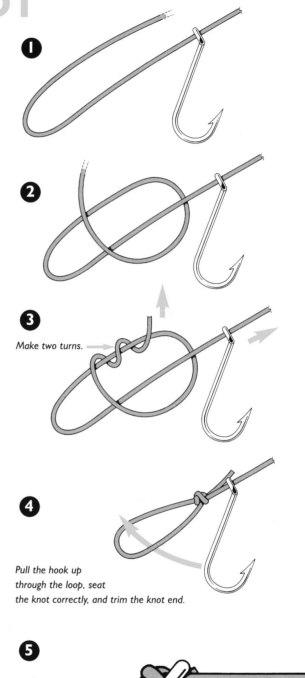

1

2

3

Make two turns.

4

Pull the hook up through the loop, seat the knot correctly, and trim the knot end.

5

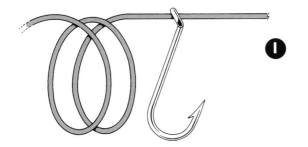

❶

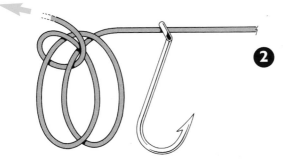

This knot ties up slightly larger than the improved turle knot but is more secure. It also gives an excellent fly presentation.

Like the improved turle knot, it is unsuitable for straight-eyed hooks.

❷

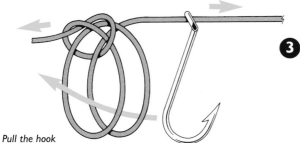

❸

Pull the hook up through the two loops, seat the knot correctly, and trim the knot end.

❹

Developed specifically for dry flies on hooks with upturned or downturned eyes, this knot must be tied with care to successfully give the precise and delicate presentation that is so vital when dry-fly fishing.

1

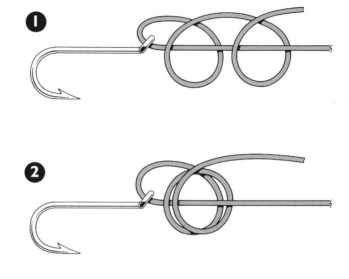

2

3

Make two turns.

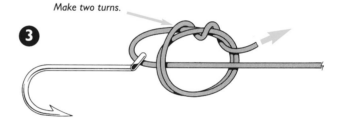

4

If the knot is tied correctly, as it is drawn up, the loops will slide back and jump over the eye of the hook. Seat the knot correctly and trim the knot end.

5

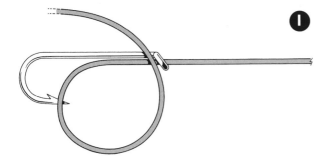

❶

An easy but exceptionally
strong method of attaching
an eyed hook to a line, the
snell is widely used by
saltwater fishermen.

❷

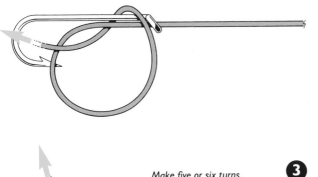

Make five or six turns.

❸

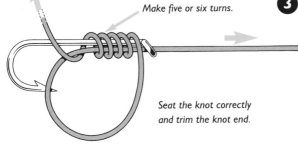

*Seat the knot correctly
and trim the knot end.*

❹

fishing knots 133

Use this knot to attach hooks with a spade end as opposed to an eyed end.

It is important to seat the knot correctly around the hook shank.

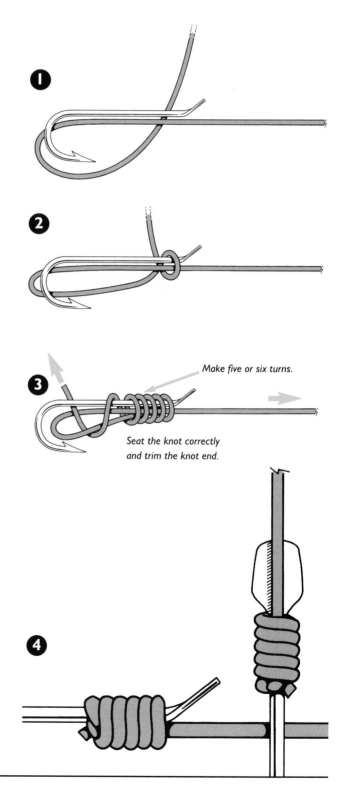

1

2

3

Make five or six turns.

Seat the knot correctly and trim the knot end.

4

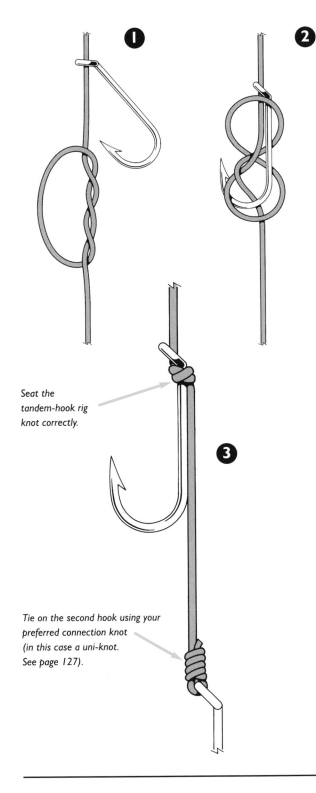

If you need a second hook attached to your line—for example, a tail hook when bait fishing—use this quick and easy tandem-hook rig.

Seat the tandem-hook rig knot correctly.

Tie on the second hook using your preferred connection knot (in this case a uni-knot. See page 127).

APPLIED
DECORATIVE
KNOTS

Decorative knotting has a long and distinguished history and is one of the oldest and most widely distributed of the folk arts. Decorative knots can be used individually or in elaborate combinations; they can be used for practical purposes or pure decoration. They have a multitude of applications, from outdoorsmanship to the worlds of fashion and interior design.

Lanyards are usually worn around the neck or attached to a belt to hold a wide variety of objects—from knives and whistles to watches and binoculars—and because the cord is left on view it is often tied with a decorative lanyard knot. Sinnets can be used to create decorative belts. One of the most popular decorative knots, the monkey's fist, has a very practical use at the end of a heaving line, the line that is thrown from boat to shore or to another vessel; decoratively it makes an attractive end to any cord. Possibly the most famous decorative knot, the Turk's head, is usually tied around cylindrical objects as pure decoration. The ocean plat is a decorative knot that is found all over the world in the form of matting, mostly aboard a ship or boat.

This chapter shows you just a few examples of how to tie and use decorative knots, but with a little imagination the possibilities for decorative knots are endless!

A lanyard is usually worn around the the neck or attached to a belt for the purpose of holding a wide variety of objects—from knives and whistles to watches and binoculars.

Lanyards have a long nautical tradition, and because the cord is left in view, sailors often decorated them with a range of elaborate knots. The knife lanyard knot is one of the most attractive and subsequently one of the most widely used.

1

2

It may help to create the first two steps of the knot around your hand, with this pattern on the front and the main loop running behind your hand.

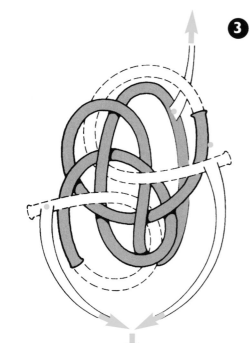

3

At first sight it may appear difficult to tie, but be patient, follow the step-by-step instructions, work the knot into its final form, and you will be rewarded with a beautiful and functional decorative knot.

4

5

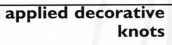

DOUBLE KNIFE
LANYARD KNOT

1

The appearance of many decorative knots can be enhanced by "doubling"— literally following the initial lead of a strand around for a second time.

The example illustrated here is a "double" version of the knife lanyard knot.

Follow steps 1, 2, and 3 of the knife lanyard knot (pages 138–9), but instead of bringing the ends out of the knot as in step 3, double both ends by leading them along the inner side of the initial lead (as in step 1, shown here).

Create step 2 and bring the ends out as shown; then draw up the knot and work it into its final form (step 3), taking care to keep the doubled strands neatly together.

2

3

140 **applied decorative knots**

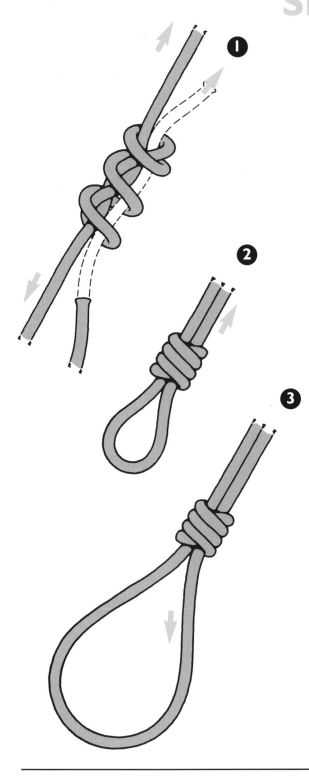

**Occasionally a sliding loop
can be a useful addition to
a lanyard.**

A simple and effective way
of achieving this is to use a
multiple overhand knot (see
page 44)—but before tightening,
slide a second strand through
the knot, as in step 1. The loop
can then be altered to the
required size.

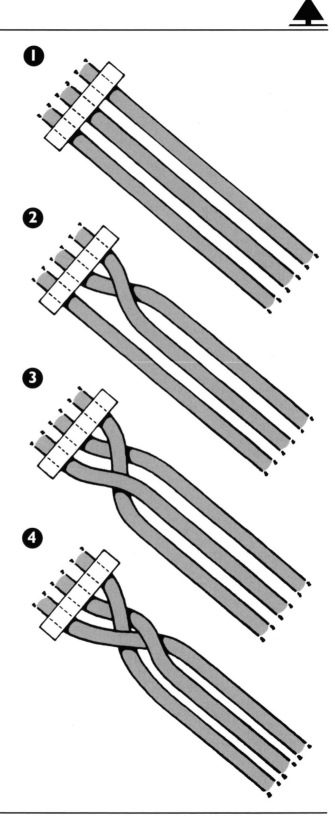

Sinnets are one or more intertwined strands that can be tied from a wide variety of materials.

They have a vast range of decorative applications, but also have many practical advantages. In the past sailors exploited the excellent "cling" and surface wear qualities of sinnet lines.

This simple, three-strand, plait or braid sinnet is also known as the English or common sinnet. Arrange the three strands as in step 1 and, if necessary, secure them in a straight line with a clip or clamp. To achieve a neat, compact sinnet, as in step 6, tighten and arrange the plait at each step of the tying.

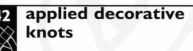

5

6

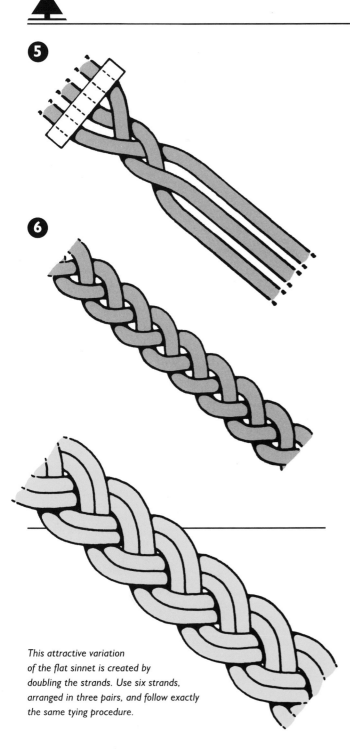

Sinnets can be finished off in a variety of ways, depending on their final use. The simplest method is by clamping or seizing with thin string and then trimming off the excess.

This attractive variation of the flat sinnet is created by doubling the strands. Use six strands, arranged in three pairs, and follow exactly the same tying procedure.

MONKEY'S FIST

The monkey's fist is a decorative knot that also has many practical uses, the most common being the knot at the end of a heaving line.

To give the monkey's fist more weight, it is often tied over a spherical object such as a heavy ball or stone. Smaller knots can be tied over golf balls; if the line is required to float, use a rubber ball. Decoratively, it makes an attractive end to any cord, and is regularly used at the end of pull cords.

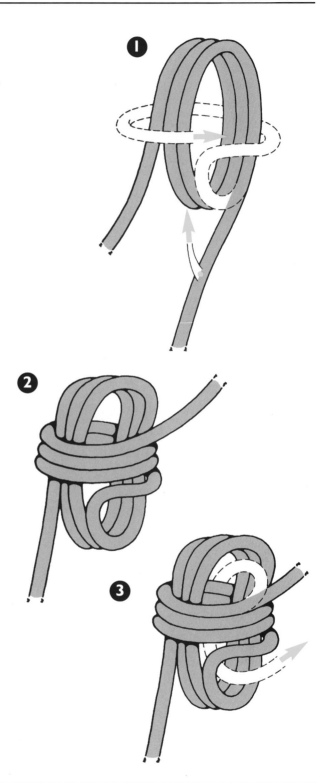

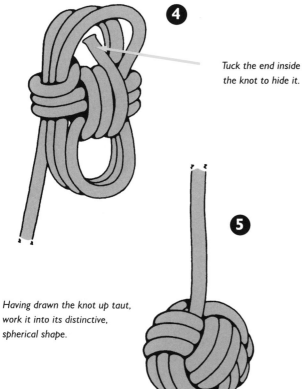

4

Tuck the end inside
the knot to hide it.

5

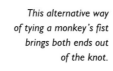

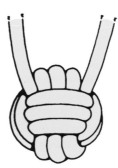

*Having drawn the knot up taut,
work it into its distinctive,
spherical shape.*

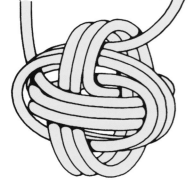

*This alternative way
of tying a monkey's fist
brings both ends out
of the knot.*

TURK'S
HEAD

Turk's head knots have long been recognized for their highly decorative attributes. Leonardo da Vinci drew them in the 15th century, and they are still widely used today.

They are usually tied around cylindrical objects—in most cases as pure decoration (for example, to decorate a tiller). But they can also serve many practical sailing purposes, and are often used to mark the position of center rudder on the ship's wheel.

1

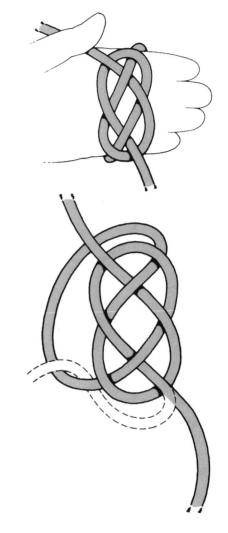

2

3

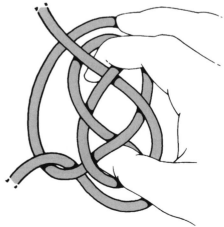

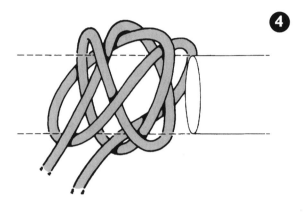

4

5

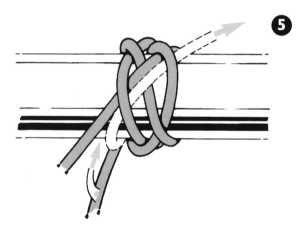

There are many recorded variations of these knots. The Turk's head shown here, a single-strand, four-lead, three-bight version, is one of the most popular. To create the finished compact knot in step 6, you'll need to work out the slack.

This is done gradually, by starting at one end of the cord and progressing right through the knot to the other end. It may also help to use a pair of thin-nose pliers.

6

This classic flat knot is found all over the world in a surprising number of situations, but its use as a mat or tread aboard ship or boat is one of the common and practical.

The size of the example shown here, which is one of the most widely used, is based on three side bights.

❶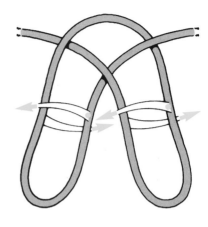

❷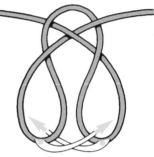

❸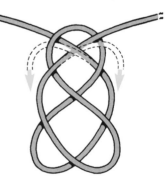

❹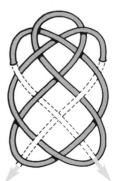

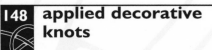

5

The pattern can be made more solid by increasing the number of times the lead is followed around, but the actual size of the knot cannot be increased.

To increase the size of the knot, the number of bights has to be increased. For example, increase to six or nine bights to create a long, narrow ocean plat for a companionway aboard ship or boat.

6

The knot can be doubled or followed around as many times as desired. It can also be left loosely formed, as shown here, or it can be tightened and made solid, as in step 7.

7

To finish, hide the ends by tucking them into the weave on the underside of the knot. If the knot is to be used as a mat, the whole structure can be greatly stengthened by sewing together all of the intersecting points with strong thread.

NET MAKING

Nets can be tied in a variety of sizes for many different uses, from fishing to storage, and it is always useful to be able to construct your own custom-sized net. One of the most popular, and important, sailing uses is safety netting between guardrails and the deck. Not only does this prevent people, especially small children, from falling overboard, but it also prevents the loss of important equipment that can often prove impossible to recover.

To construct a net you will require a reel of good netting twine, a net needle, and a piece of wood with straight edges.

A net needle will make it easy to thread the twine and save you from having to pull the whole line through at each turn.

A wooden straightedge will enable you to hold and check the mesh to give a uniform pattern.

1

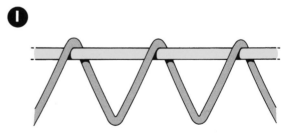

2

3

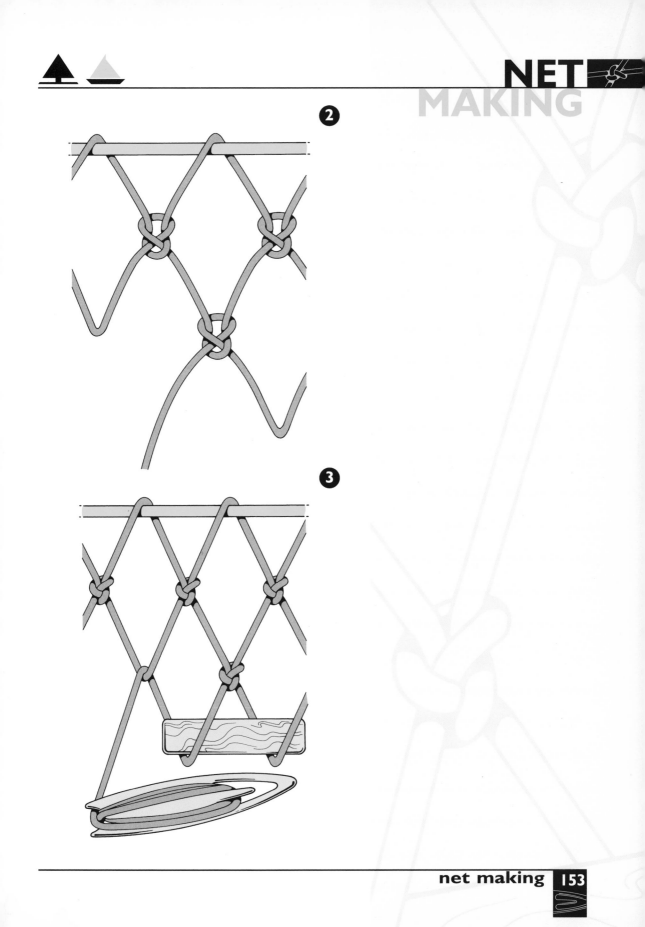

GLOSSARY

Astern. At or toward the rear part of a boat or the reversing maneuver of a vessel, as in: full speed astern!

Backing line. High-breaking-strain monofilament or braided line used under the fly line on a reel to bulk out the spool. Also used as additional line when the fly line is stripped off the reel by a fish making a long run.

Belay. To secure a rope or line with figure-eight turns around a cleat.

Bend. The action of tying two ropes together by their ends. Also the name given to the group of knots that are used to tie lines to each other or to some other object.

Bight. The slack section of the rope between the working end and the standing end. The term is particularly used when this section of the rope is formed into a loop or turned back on itself. Knots tied "in the bight" or "on the bight" do not require you to use the ends in the tying process.

Bollard. A large fixed post made of iron or wood for mooring a boat to.

Bow. The front end of a boat.

Braid. To interweave several strands.

Breaking strength or **strain.** The manufacturer's estimate of the load that will cause a rope to part. This calculation is based on strength of a dry line under a steady pull; it generally takes no account of wetness, wear and tear, knots, or shock loading. Lines are weaker when worn, wet, or knotted; the manufacturer's estimate cannot, therefore, be regarded as a safe working load.

Butt. The thicker part of a leader, usually monofilament, that is attached to the fly line.

Cable. A rope of large diameter: anchor warp or chain.

Cable-laid. Rope formed of three right-handed hawsers laid up left-handed to make a larger, nine-stranded rope or cable.

Chafe. To make or become worn or frayed by rubbing.

Cleat. A T-shaped fitting on which a rope or line can be secured.

Cord. The name given to several tightly twisted yarns making a line with a diameter of less than $1/2$ inch.

Cordage. Collective name for ropes and cords; especially used to describe the ropes in a ship's rigging.

Core. The inner or central part found in ropes and sinnets of more than three strands, and in most braided lines. Formed from a bundle of parallel strands or loosely twisted yarn running the length of the rope, or the central part of a monkey's fist knot, inserted to add weight.

Dropper. Short length of monofilament, joined or tied into the leader to attach additional flies or tackle.

Eye. A circle or loop attached or formed at the end of a hook or item of tackle, to which line is attached or a loop formed at the end of a length of rope.

Fender. A cushion of flexible material positioned on the sides of boats to prevent damage when tying up or mooring.

Fid. Tapered wooden pin used to work or loosen strands of rope.

Fly line. A coated nylon, Dacron, or PVC line specifically developed to cast an artificial fly attached to a leader.

Fray. To unravel, especially the end of a piece of rope.

Grommet or **grummet.** A ring, usually made of metal or twisted rope, that is used to fasten the edge of a sail to its stay, hold an oar in place, etc.

Hawser. A rope or cable, 5 to 24 inches in circumference, large enough for towing or mooring.

Heaving line. A line with a weighted knot tied at one end that is attached to another heavier line and is thrown from boat to shore or to another vessel. The purpose of the line is to draw behind it a heavier line that will be used for tying up or mooring.

Hitch. Knot made to secure a rope to a ring, spar, etc., or to another rope.

Lanyard. A short length of rope or cord made decorative with knots and sinnets. Used to secure personal objects; usually worn around the neck or attached to a belt.

Lay. The direction, right- or left-handed, of the twist in the strands that form a rope.

Leader. The tapered length of nylon that forms the connection between a fly line and a fly. It may be tapered mechanically (knotless), or created by joining sections of line with reducing diameters.

GLOSSARY

Line. Generic name for cordage with no specific purpose, although it can describe a particular use (clothesline, fishing line, etc.).

Loop. Part of a rope that is bent so that it comes together across itself.

Lure. A term to describe artificial baits.

Make fast. To secure a rope or line to a cleat, etc.

Monofilament. Strong and flexible single-strand nylon line.

Nip. The binding pressure within a knot that stops it from slipping.

Over and under. Description of the weave in knots such as the Turk's head.

Plain-laid rope. Three-strand rope laid (twisted) to the right.

Plait or **plat.** Pronounced *plat*. To intertwine strands in a pattern.

Port. The left-hand side of a boat looking forward.

Reeve. The act of threading or passing a rope through an aperture such as a ring, block, or cleat.

Retractor. A spring-loaded spool of cord, usually pinned to clothing, to attach items such as scissors.

Rope. Strong, thick cord more than 1 inch in circumference made from twisted strands of fiber, wire, etc.

Running rigging. Rope or wire used to control the sails.

Seat or **Seated.** A term used to describe the process of knot formation.

Seizing. To bind two ropes or cords together.

Shank. The straight part of a hook.

Sinker. Any weight, usually lead, that is attached to a fishing line.

Sinnet or **sennet.** Braided cordage (flat, round, or square) formed from three to nine cords.

Small stuff. Thin cordage, twine, string, rope, or line that has a circumference of less than 1 inch, or a diameter of less than $1/2$ inch.

Snell. To tie a hook by wrapping line around its shank or straight part.

Spade end. The flattened end of the shank of a hook.

Spar. A mast, boom, or gaff.

Splice. To join the ends of rope by interweaving the strands.

Standing end. The short area at the end of the standing part of the rope.

Standing part. The part of the rope that is fixed and under tension (as opposed to the free working end with which the knot is tied).

Starboard. The right-hand side of a boat looking forward.

Stern. The back of a boat.

Stopper knot. Any terminal knot used to bind the end of a line, cord, or rope to prevent it from unraveling and also to provide a decorative end.

Strand. Yarns twisted together in the opposite direction to the yarn itself. Rope made from strands (rope that is not braided) is called laid line.

Swivel. An item of tackle to prevent twists in the line, used when spinning a lure.

Tag end. The part of the line in which the knot is tied and then the excess is trimmed off.

Taut. Tightly stretched.

Thimble. A metal or plastic eye used to shape an eye splice and prevent chafe.

Tippet. The thin terminal section of the leader, to which the fly is tied.

Turn. One complete revolution of one line around another.

Twine. Thin line of various types for various uses, as in whipping twine, etc.

Warp. A general term for mooring ropes, anchor cable, etc.

Whipping. Tightly wrapping small stuff around the end of a cord or rope to prevent it from fraying.

Work (to). To draw and shape a knot; to make the final arrangement.

Working end. The part of the rope or cord used actively in tying a knot. The opposite of the standing end.

Yarn. The basic element of rope or cord formed from artificial or synthetic filaments or natural fibers.

CONVERSION CHARTS

Linear Measure		
0.25 inch	=	0.6 cm
0.5 inch	=	1.25 cm
1 inch	=	2.54 cm
2 inches	=	5.08 cm
4 inches	=	10.16 cm
6 inches	=	15.25 cm
8 inches	=	20.32 cm
10 inches	=	25.40 cm
12 inches (1 foot)	=	30.48 cm
2 feet	=	0.61 m
3 feet (1 yard)	=	0.91 m
5 feet	=	1.52 m
10 feet	=	3.05 m

Temperature		
Celsius		Fahrenheit
-17.8°	=	0°
-10°	=	14°
0°	=	32°
10°	=	50°
20°	=	68°
30°	=	86°
40°	=	104°
50°	=	122°
60°	=	140°
70°	=	158°
80°	=	176°
90°	=	194°
100°	=	212°

Measures of Weight		
1 lb	=	450 g
2 lb	=	900 g
5 lb	=	2.25 kg
10 lb	=	4.5 kg
20 lb	=	9 kg
50 lb	=	23 kg
100 lb	=	46 kg

Note: The conversion factors are not exact.

They are given only to the accuracy likely to be needed in everyday calculations.

PERSONAL KNOT
NOTES

PERSONAL KNOT NOTES

PERSONAL KNOT
NOTES